O9-BHL-707

Born to Be a Blessing

A Parent's Guide to Raising Christian Children

BORN TO BE A BLESSING
A PARENT'S GUIDE TO RAISING CHRISTIAN CHILDREN

Copyright © 2009 by Abingdon Press
All rights reserved.

No part of this work may be reproduced or transmitted in any form or by any means, electronic or mechanical, including photocopying, recording, or by any information storage or retrieval system, except as may be expressly permitted by the 1976 Copyright Act or in writing from the publisher. Requests for permission should be submitted in writing to:
Rights and Permissions, The United Methodist Publishing House, 201 Eighth Avenue, South, P.O. Box 801, Nashville, TN 37202-0801; faxed to 615-749-6128; or e-mailed to *permissions@abingdonpress.com.*

Scripture quotations are taken from the New Revised Standard Version of the Bible, copyright 1989, Division of Christian Education of the National Council of the Churches of Christ in the United States of America. Used by permission.
All rights reserved.

ISBN: 978-1-426-70676-9

Photo of Myrtle Felkner on the back cover and on page 8 by Michael Browns.
Photos on pages 11, 15, 17, 50, 57, 85, 90, 122 © Design Pics, Inc.
Photos on pages 22, 34, 38, 69, 76, 79, 93, 102, 109, 111, 113, 115, 129, 135, 141 © Liquid Library.
Art on page 40 by Robert S. Jones, © 2008 Cokesbury.
Photo on page 89 by Stephen Gardner.

09 10 11 12 13 14 15 16 17 18 —10 9 8 7 6 5 4 3 2 1
PRINTED IN THE UNITED STATES OF AMERICA

Born to Be a Blessing

A Parent's Guide to Raising Christian Children

Myrtle E. Felkner

Abingdon Press

Nashville

CONTENTS

Dedication

To the Potato Peeler Guy and Our Children

FOREWORD

PARENTING: THE MOST IMPORTANT JOB
WE WILL EVER HAVE

What a challenging and important position we have if we are among those with children in our lives! Whether you are a parent, a grandparent, or a teacher who guides children, this book is meant to inspire and perhaps even to enrich some of your day-to-day contacts with the young. There is no more challenging task than faithful parenting as we seek to make God known in our families.

Making the most of every moment is the name of the game. The time that modern families have together may be very limited, and it may be that your children do not see you in the better parts of the day. This author and parent does not view parenting as a process of setting down rules, seeing those rules are obeyed, or demanding proscribed behavior; in other words, ruling the roost through demands for compliance rather than cooperation as a unit seeking to live in tune with God. Granted, children must be aware of family expectations and boundaries, and God must ever be a part of our growing together as a family; and that means seeking God and God's will for every detail in our lives.

Aren't those details wonderful! Families who add humor, adventure, active learning, and imagination to their God-seeking will find God in every detail, every experience. Of course, study of the Bible is important; its lessons are primary and are repeated often in our lives as guidance and inspiration. Study of nature, its creatures, its wondrous unity, draw us closer to the God of creation. Knowing Jesus impacts every relationship, both inside and outside the family. As we grow in our own knowledge and practice of faithful discipleship, our children are nurtured in their faith.

I want to express my own appreciation and love for my partner in raising our children, The Potato Peeler Guy, and for our children, Barbara, Joan, and Bill, and their families. A special thanks is extended to Joan, who helped her computer-challenged mother to pull this manuscript together.

Myrtle E. Felkner

Photo by Michael Browns

INTRODUCTION

Every child is born to be a blessing. As parents, most of us want to respond positively to all the privileges of parenthood. None is more important than guiding and nurturing the child in faith formation and development.

This book speaks to that privilege from years of experience and from the viewpoint of parent-child relationships that respond to the child's world. Whether the child is involved in creative play, has had a bad day, or is simply searching for answers to a number of childhood's dilemmas, this book offers some insight into faithful living. Parents will deal with areas of the child's life such as self-control, truth-telling, sibling rivalry, generosity, decision-making, heroes and heroines, all set within the context of our faith in God and our desire to live as loving, faithful disciples of Jesus.

Each chapter begins with a verse of Scripture and ends with questions for meditation and discussion. Wonderful stories of real children are included in every chapter as the author shares from her decades of working with children in a variety of settings. Positive and practical problem-solving is illustrated; humor and moments of joy are shared. This book should call forth from readers a response of hope and energy for the best job of all—raising Christian children.

PART ONE
FALL
TURNING LEAVES

THE DIPLOMATIC COFFEE CAN
BIBLE READING: EPHESIANS 6:1-4

I paused hesitantly at the door of the Klubhouse. My eleven-year-old hosts lent a hand as I climbed over the twisted limb of an old pear tree and entered their castle. Here at the tree-stump table, seated on tree-stump chairs, we enjoyed soft drinks while the boys pointed out such unique features as the upstairs recliner, the air-raid shelter, the mailbox, even a doorbell (a can of rocks—very effective). This spacious Klubhouse extended over part of an abandoned orchard, whose twisted or fallen apple and pear trees offered terrific possibilities. The boys built with salvaged tin and lumber, fashioning a retreat to warm the heart of even a grandmother.

I suppose it was the air-raid shelter, whose roof was a discarded chick brooder, that stimulated my thinking. Obviously, these fellows were living in response to world events. I gave them a flag to fly over the air-raid shelter, and I ventured the opinion that there would be mail in the mailbox before too long. In an envelope marked "Diplomatic MAIL. Open at ONCE," I enclosed the following note: "I have had word that the King of Slobovia is planning to capture your flag and occupy the Klubhouse. I am willing to negotiate the peace between the Klubhouse and Slobovia."

The kids and I had often played these games. My expectation was that I would be appointed ambassador or UN Peacemaker at the very least. To my surprise, the message that appeared in my own mailbox was a terse, "Bring 'em on." When I checked with the boys, they assured me that they had stored up an ample supply of ammunition—green peas, walnuts, and hedge apples. Any Slobs who tried to capture the flag could be easily resisted.

Enter the Diplomatic Coffee Can. Two chocolate bars accompanied an official request from the Slobs to build their own capitol at the far end of the orchard. Would chocolate bars be considered adequate rent? I placed the Diplomatic Coffee Can in their mailbox and waited an anxious week for a reply. As of now, we are still negotiating; and I am cautiously hopeful.

* * * * * * * * * * * * * * * * * * * *

Imaginative games are nothing new to our children and grandchildren. We have delightful memories of sandbox castles being stormed by Sir Knight on his trusted tractor. We have turned the family room into a multicultural village. An igloo of sheets is Alaska, complete with polar bear stuffed toys; Africa is under the table, where we confine the tigers and lions; India is in the far corner, with a music box and elephants and monkeys.

Parents and other adults who play with children, structured play as well as imaginative games, will quickly discover the developmental benefits of such play for their children. Dr. Howard Gardner, author of *Frames of Mind,* has identified eight ways in which we gather and process information. Play, which is the work of children, reinforces these intelligences, enabling us to function and learn in a variety of ways. Children who experience learning in multiple ways grow in their self-confidence, accept and appreciate their identity, and are motivated to move on to deeper ways of learning and playing.

My grandson and I stood on a hill during our timber hike, looking over the land around us. We tried to imagine what Kyle's great-great-great-grandfather felt and thought as he stood on that hill for the first time 150 years ago. Did he see wood for a house and fences? wild berries, mushrooms? Did he spot deer at this place, possum, raccoon, pheasant, turkeys? Whatever he saw and felt, Grandfather put down roots and raised a large family. How was his life different from ours on these very same acres? We came up with a list of more than one hundred differences.

History is not the story of battles and conquerors. It is the story of humankind and how it lived, worshiped, coped, experienced the presence of God in the everyday work and play of life. Sometimes the children and I contrive elaborate board games that contain every setback we have had all week; sometimes we make secret trails through the woods; and sometimes we examine social issues through simulation. Such play connects us with the past and the future and helps us see that God is present in all of life.

The fact that we do it together adds value to our play. When parents and their children play together, the children become increasingly aware that their welfare, their safety, their interests, their hopes, and their frustrations are known and respected by the adults. Children also learn to be helpful and cooperative, partnering in this event we share. After all, it is obvious that Grandma will never learn to skateboard well without attentive supervision and help. Time spent with our children is never wasted; if time is spent in play, we add both pleasure and purpose.

Uh-oh. The Diplomatic Coffee Can is back. The boys suggest that a fair rent would be two chocolate bars and two soft drinks. In addition to orchard space, they would also grant access to the creek. I think Slobovia will go for that.

Questions for Discussion and Meditation

1. What would you need to give up, adjust, or neglect to find time to play with your children?

2. How would the benefits of family play outweigh the sacrifices?

3. How does "The Diplomatic Coffee Can" adhere to Ephesians 6:1-4?

4. When is "play" also "instruction"?

5. What are the holy points in the daily news to which your children are responding today? (Note the "bring 'em on" comment.) Do your children express opinions about current news?

6. Do you agree or disagree?

7. Where do you see God acting in history?

SIBLING RIVALRY
BIBLE READING: ZECHARIAH 7:8-10; EPHESIANS 4:1-3

Five kittens played their kitten games in our yard. One seemed to dominate all the others, even when two of his littermates approached him stealthily from different directions. Kitten One sent them scurrying for the barn, then laid down in the sun, ears up, alert to the possibility of another challenger.

* *

Sounds just like your kids, right?

Sibling rivalry seems a part of the human family as far back as Cain and Abel, Jacob and Esau, or Joseph and his brothers. Such rivalry can lead to violence, as it sometimes did in those early Bible stories.

Fortunately, there are ways in which parents can minimize rivalry between or among their children without resorting to violence themselves.

A neighbor of mine left her family more than twenty years ago with hard feelings toward her sister. Though her family knows the city where she resides, my neighbor will neither accept telephone calls nor allow her parents to see their grandchildren. This is not a unique circumstance. Almost all of us know of broken relationships that have their roots in childhood sibling rivalry. What can we do about it?

AVOID COMPARISON

"You can do better in school; your sister has all A's. I wish you would pay attention like Asta does." "You just don't have music in your bones like Jason does." "If you would keep your room as neat as Margaret's, I would feel more like taking you to the movie."

No wonder the poor child feels inferior and, in addition, would like to give his or her sibling a good swat. Think about the Jacob and Esau Bible story. Isaac admired his hunter son, the hairy and robust Esau. On the other hand, Rebekah admired the smooth and suave Jacob—perhaps because he reminded her of her brother, Laban. Do you suppose she rubbed it in that Jacob was more like her family? Whenever we compare a child to the embarrassment or disadvantage of another child, we are making a deposit for sibling rivalry, either now or in the future.

STOP PUTTING LABELS ON PEOPLE, ESPECIALLY CHILDREN

"You are a rotten kid. You'll never amount to anything." "I wish I had a dime for every lie you have told me." "Stand up; don't be such a slouch."

Labels are harmful and may lead to the child's belief that indeed there is something wrong or weird about himself or herself. Children may then strike back at the nearest, most vulnerable people—their siblings.

An old song urges us to "accentuate the positive." There are good and worthy things to say about any child. Do not be dishonest, but search for a characteristic or talent you can affirm. Yesterday, I saw a young man who had been a very naughty little boy. When his teenage daughter learned I had been his Sunday school teacher, her eyes widened in disbelief. "He was very creative," I assured her. "I had to work hard to keep him out of mischief." We three enjoyed a good laugh; and as they moved away, I heard him say, "See, I was too a good boy." He was to me. Creative is not the same as bad.

IDENTIFY AND CORRECT FAVORITISM

Although Joseph was probably too braggy to be a pleasant younger brother, he was himself a victim of his father's favoritism. From the beginning, Jacob loved Rachel and merely tolerated Leah, the first wife. He carried that favoritism over to his large family. Of them all, he loved Joseph best. The jealousy and anger that this generated in Jacob's family is no different from what we can expect as a result of favoritism today. (For a complete reading and understanding of this Bible story, read Genesis 29–37.)

ARTICULATE FAMILY VALUES

Be sure the guidelines are clearly articulated. "Our family doesn't use tobacco, alcohol, or drugs." "Our family eats the evening meal together." "We are musical people; and we may each choose an instrument to learn, if we wish." "No television or computer games until homework is done." Whatever the rules that express your values, be sure they are understood. Rigidity sometimes gives way to circumstances, of course, but those must be negotiated. Your children will get along better if they know exactly where you stand and what you expect of every family member. Work together, play together, worship together, and respect one another.

Enjoy one another! Have fun. Families are more likely to be bonded by spending time together. Time in recreation, time pursuing mutual goals, time worshiping and serving others is time that will be fondly remembered. Small family tiffs will be forgotten, and children will grow up emotionally healthier in families where sibling rivalry is minimized by the watchfulness and loving efforts of parents.

Questions for Discussion and Meditation

1. Review Ephesians 4:1-3. How do you maintain "the unity of the Spirit in the bond of peace"? How does this apply to family life? Does peace come at any price? How does this Bible verse apply to congregational life?

2. Invite your whole family to make a list of family values. Some values you will insist upon as part of your parental responsibilities. Other values may be suggested and debated by all members. Be open to suggestions that you may not have considered. Engage your children in discussion of healthy families as opposed to dysfunctional families. Name examples of each from your Bible studies.

3. Sing together "Let There Be Peace on Earth" by Sy Miller and Jill Jackson. Talk about the meaning of each phrase. Could your family use this song as a prayer each day?

WHEN CHILDREN ARE THE RELUCTANT TRAVELERS
BIBLE READING: HEBREWS 13:1-2

My friend was aghast when I told her that my parents as tenant farmers had moved to four separate neighborhoods before I was in high school. I loved it.

"Loved it!" she exclaimed. "How could you? My folks moved every year or two, and I always felt like a transient."

I loved exploring new farms, walking in new fields and woods, claiming a new room, hiding in new attics, finding new hidden nests of eggs when the chickens were let out in the spring. What's not to love?

For many children such constant upheaval, especially in emergency situations, is very hard to handle and can result in feelings of abandonment and insecurity. The source of security and identity for me and my siblings was always the small Danish-American church to which we returned, no matter where we lived. Parents who must uproot their families due to jobs or other circumstances do not always have such a lodestar. What factors can help us give confidence, security, and pleasure to children who are "reluctant travelers"?

Moving may indeed be traumatic. We have only to think of tsunami and hurricane victims to know that. Others may begin the move happily; but like the Israelites in the wilderness, they soon tire of the changes. We can only imagine how the children felt on that long exodus from Egypt, some of whom spent a lifetime wandering in the wilderness. Eventually, the nomadic people had roomy tents, some with fine carpets, and often stayed for weeks or months until the grazing for their animals was depleted. The security of the children rested in the daylong proximity of parents and familiar relatives, tents, and animals.

Reluctant travelers today are children and youth who are uprooted from schools, social or cultural groups, houses, and neighborhoods. They must not only cope with the unfamiliar but must find ways to assimilate new experiences in positive ways.

HOW CAN WE HELP?

- Do not minimize or ignore feelings of alienation or abandonment in children, even though they may not verbalize those feelings. Accompany your children to their new school to visit with the principal and meet teachers the first day. Accompany your children to the new Sunday school, and offer help to their classes. Perhaps bringing a treat, assisting with learning activities in young children's classes, or providing transportation or support for field trips would be welcome assistance and would help your child bridge the gap between the old and the new.

- Encourage your child to make new friends. This is not easy when groups of children have been together for several years. The newcomer is not always immediately accepted. Find ways to integrate new interests in your child's life. New friends can be found through dance lessons or community sports programs. These activities do not guarantee new friends, but common interests and proximity will help.

- Explore as a family what your new city, town, or community has to offer. Introduce your children to the art center, the museum, the library, the lake, the trails for biking and hiking, the nature center, the county fair—whatever is available. As your children begin to feel familiar with their environment, their sense of belonging will grow.

- Share your own feelings. Are you missing old friends, the old job? Explain to younger children that you are making the best of it and working toward your family's future welfare. Explain clearly and kindly that everyone in the family has had to leave something behind; but that what is ahead can be very good, too. Acknowledge feelings of loneliness, but do not dwell on them.

- If you have been displaced because of disasters such as flooding or fire, reassure your children concerning their safety and point out the many people who love them and are willing to help them.

- Roleplay other situations and circumstances. What did the children do on that long desert walk with Moses? How did they feel about leaving all that was familiar in Egypt? Did the children watch as Joshua marched around Jericho? Did they play games or sing songs about their hero Joshua? When children recognize that other children have successfully negotiated their way through difficult travels or moves, they realize that they, too, can make changes that add positive value to their lives.

- Suggest that your children keep journals or write stories, songs, or jingles about their experiences. Younger children who have experienced traumatic moves sometimes can express their feelings by drawing pictures. Take turns with your child adding new figures to a very large drawing. Stick figures of people are fine. Large voluminous trees and box-like houses or schools may recall memories, perhaps chuckles. This sharing of feelings through drawing and song relieves anxiety and promotes honest facing of memories or problems.

- Work together on the big projects. Even a five-year-old can scrub a birdbath, paint a flower trellis, bathe or feed the dog, or wash the baby's toys. Children who invest in family activities gain feelings of self-worth and value to the family unit, which are especially important during times of transition.

- Sing, play, bake, explore, play games. Invite neighbors for coffee or play time.

But through it all, of course, be aware that if your child suffers severe depression, you may need to seek family counseling. Right now the best thing parents can do for the "reluctant travelers" is to assure them always that God loves them and that you love them. Who knows what wonderful thing may happen tomorrow?

Questions for Discussion and Meditation

1. Consider the "reluctant travelers" in your church, community, or school system. How can you and your children honor the biblical mandate of love and inclusiveness to strangers? How do you choose what is wise, even safe? Plan an event that will welcome the reluctant traveler as well as teach your own children to make others comfortable.

2. Who are the newcomers in this congregation? Who is missing and has "moved on"? How can you offer support and understanding to each group?

3. Many homeless people lived in box-like shacks along the river, until one shack burned due to a faulty propane heater. City workers arrived with bulldozers and cleared the spot as a safety issue. As many people as possible were accommodated at a shelter; others were left to camp under bridges and in doorways. Can you think of other solutions? What would Jesus do?

THEOLOGY 1001: WHY NOT?
BIBLE READING: DEUTERONOMY 6:5-7

My kindergarten friend bore down on me. "Myrtle," he said, "if God made dinosaurs, why don't we still have any?" His dad, who was following him closely, gave me an expressive shrug of the shoulders as I sought for just the right words. "No one knows for sure," I said, "but I think God just saw that smaller animals would be more useful for the other creatures of the earth."

"Why?" he asked. This was one focused kid. I felt I was caught teaching Theology 1001 without a lesson plan.

THEOLOGY FOR KIDS? WHY NOT?

Theology is not just an abstract subject to be pondered by bishops and other clergy. My dictionary defines *theology* as "the study of God and the relationship between God and the universe." Put into more simple terms for children, *Theology* is "thinking about God." Most children who have been to church or Sunday school do a fair amount of that on their own, as shown by my kindergarten friend. Guiding the God-journey is one of the awesome privileges of parenthood.

A little boy found it hard to observe all the beautiful things that his grandma was pointing out as they walked in the woods. Finally, he suggested, "Grandma, when you see something beautiful that God made, just say, 'Stop!' and I will stop and look. But right now, I have to look at the ground so I won't step in something bad." This little guy had been around his daddy's cattle long enough to know that there are hazards in walking around the farm. Nevertheless, he was reluctant to miss anything beautiful that God had made. We can all find those beautiful things, from city sidewalks to well-worn deer trails approaching rural corn fields. Teaching our children to appreciate God's creation helps them cherish the relationship between God and the universe.

But where is God in the war scenes they see daily on the television screen, the abuse of others that occurs around them, the neglect or irresponsibility that may even be happening in their own lives? Why doesn't God just put a stop to it?

These are legitimate questions for all of us, especially for children. You will not be able to ignore them. The children are "doing" theology: thinking about God and attempting to interpret their world in God's terms.

God made human beings with free will. For children, that means the right to choose. Some choices are age specific. They may choose what to wear to school, but they may not choose whether they go to school. Once the practical limitations of childhood are clear, parents may begin to talk with children about the consequences of choice.

Because human beings have made unfortunate, even tragic, choices, there are wars in the world. Because human beings have been selfish, even greedy, there are hungry children in the world. God works as we pray that our hearts may be turned to Christ and that peace may rule the world. God is also at work when children practice kindness and are helpful to others.

My Sunday school class was puzzled when I asked them about the requirements of love. On the way to church, I saw a very dirty, unkempt person staggering drunkenly around the town square, spitting and cursing. *Am I required by God to love this person?*

Obviously, these kids did not know what to say. They wanted to say *no*, such a person was not loveable; and they certainly could not love a dirty, drunken, cursing, spitting individual. They had been taught to avoid such people, not to converse or be in contact with them. Still, the children wanted to please their teacher, and they knew in their hearts that God loved that person. Choices, choices!

Perhaps it was hard for the children to believe that God wanted the same things for this person that God wants for us and our families: shelter, good food, protection, love. Even an education? dance lessons? an alto saxophone? We left class thinking about God, intending to ask our families what they thought about this dilemma. *Whole families theologizing! Think of it!*

My granddaughter seemed pleased that God had made spiders with eight legs. But we questioned why God had made it so, as we observed Herman scampering around the bathtub. Surely, four legs would have been easier to handle. We could only conclude that God was not only all-powerful and all-knowing, but that God was also all-wise. Surely, there was a reason for eight legs, and someday we would ask God!

We learned much from Herman while he was a guest in the bathtub. Would the fruit of an osage orange tree really repel spiders, as our mothers and grandmothers had taught us? Nope. Herman climbed onto the hedge ball we placed in the tub and seemed quite satisfied with himself. So if hedge balls (osage oranges) did not repel spiders, what good were they? Why had God sent such an abundance of hedge balls to southern Iowa?

We now conclude that just as new medicines are discovered from some of the trees and plants of the jungles, perhaps humankind has yet to unfold some wonderful secret that God has locked in the hedge ball. We chop one open to look, but we see nothing significant. God is all-wise and keeps the secret hidden for awhile longer.

Theology 1001 constantly reminds us that our world is full of God's wonderful secrets and magnificent possibilities. Children who are guided in their God-search have begun a fulfilling lifetime journey, one full of both mystery and discovery. It is our job as parents and teachers to guide and encourage their questions and delight in their discoveries.

Questions for Discussion and Meditation

1. Theological reflection can happen any time, even when a spider takes up residence in the bathtub. We cannot miss the opportunities each day to "talk with our children when we are at home and when we are away" about God and God's awesome creation. When do you and your children think about God together, other than prayer time? What mysteries have you explored? What have your children learned about God through conversation and exploration of the world where you are?

2. How about those dinosaurs? Science has put forward various theories concerning their disappearance. Did God cause them to disappear? If so, what else might God zap at any time? Could there have been natural or circumstantial causes?

3. God created an orderly world. Sometimes, however, we feel that things have gone amuck. Why are there physically challenged children? Why do rivers flood and mountains crumble? How do we reflect on these questions when a child asks?

WHO WILL LEAD THEM ARIGHT?
BIBLE READING: PSALM 25:4-5

Sixteen gorgeous bluebirds fluttered to a landing at my birdbath. Never before had I seen so many bluebirds in one place and never one so close to my west window! Cold weather was nipping at our heels on this day, and I was glad this flock of migrating birds had blessed my life.

I am reminded again of William Cullen Bryant's "To a Waterfowl." The poet, spotting a migrating bird, had felt reassured that the One who guided the waterfowl across the trackless sky to its safe haven in a warmer climate would also guide the poet aright in "the long way that I must tread alone." *Surely, the mysteries of bird and animal migration intrigue us; but the larger question remains, will we also trust God to "lead our steps aright"?*

Parents, teachers, and all who love children are concerned about character formation in our young people. As Christians, we nurture the hope that each one might come to know God through Jesus Christ and, like the poet, might be confident in a future under the care of God, who indeed will lead our steps aright.

A little girl named Rachel told me, "I don't care if I have a party, because I love God, and I have Jesus and my family in my heart." This caring child had recently celebrated her adoption with cupcakes for everyone in her class at school. Leading her steps aright is now a tremendous privilege for her new parents, for the church, and for the caring adults who have even a small part in her life. Obviously, Rachel is off to a good start. She has God and Jesus in her heart.

Most parents and grandparents are well aware of the multiple temptations that lie in wait for any child. The most basic step we can take to promote Christian values with our children is to share experiences and to talk, talk, talk. We communicate to children that there are often difficult choices in life. Which way would Jesus want us to go? What ramifications and consequences may be involved with each choice? Which choice advances our understanding and empathy with others in our world?

- A third-grade boy became addicted to drugs through contacts on the school playground.

- A beloved pastor has sought help for a gambling addiction.

- A popular physician has illegally obtained numerous drugs to treat his own pain.

- A political leader has pleaded guilty to dishonesty and fraud.

Our daily newspapers are filled with these stories. Children must be prepared from their earliest years to understand the nature of God's promise to lead our steps aright.

First, children learn to trust God through their experiences of trusting their primary caretakers. Parents, grandparents, teachers, child-care workers—whoever has authority over a child—must be trustworthy, period. How can children learn to trust God if they experience the loss of security that comes when they distrust those close to them?

A child with instability in her life said to me, "I don't want to listen about Jesus, and I don't want to listen about God because I already know all that stuff." Obviously, this child was having a bad day. She has had to handle both grief and change in her short life, and some days she is more likely to feel cross than to feel secure. The task of the caring adults in her life is to assure her of the prevenient love of God. God has been loving her and searching for her heart before she is ever consciously aware of God's presence. She is struggling to accept that God means only good for her life.

Children also need to see Bible stories and Bible truths lived out in the realities of their own lives. How does the Bible story of Jonah apply to them? There is little likelihood that these children will ever spend several days in the belly of a big fish, so perhaps the real lessons are that God can do magnificent things, such as saving Nineveh; and sometimes even a child or a very reluctant believer can be God's chosen agent of change. Each child must then consider: *What is God preparing me to do? Will I trust God to lead my steps aright?*

Finally, we need to help children develop coping skills when things go badly. This does not mean that God has deserted us. Although most of us can philosophically accept that sometimes things go amuck, the wound is there, and we need healing. Children heal when they feel our empathy, when we have taken this problem to God together, and when the situation is corrected insofar as that is possible. Adults should always be ready to listen to even the most minor of a child's concerns.

My neighbor boy insisted that a car along our busy highway near his neighborhood had deliberately swerved to hit and kill his dog. This boy's grief was so intense, his anger at the driver so fierce that it was days before he could even begin to face life without his companion. Long bicycle rides, timber hikes, and numerous tree houses built with a friend eased his loneliness. His pastor and his friends at church helped him to let go and let God and give up his desire for awesome revenge. There is One whom we can trust to heal our wounds. This child went on to hold an important and confidential position as an adult; he channeled his desire for revenge into a lifetime of fighting evil. God, indeed, led this boy's steps aright.

And so it is with all of us—birds, beasts, human beings, crawly things. Each one is under God's eye. I hurry to put out some mealy worms for the bluebirds, in the event that they come this way again. And as I do so, I reflect again on our God's gracious goodness, knowing that God is there and will lead our steps aright.

Questions for Discussion and Meditation

1. There are both awful and awesome stories in the lives of many children. On what evidence do you base your belief in God's prevenient love for every child?

2. Read again the listing of news articles about the young boy, the pastor, the physician, the political leader. Did God fail to "lead them aright"? What happened there? What can we learn from events such as these?

3. What influences your family the most: television or the Bible? Do you need to make changes? How can you do that peaceably?

EVERY MINUTE COUNTS
BIBLE READING: MATTHEW 18:1-5, 10-14

My mischievous young friend and I were walking to the church kitchen to get the treats for a large group of youngsters. Clearly, this fellow was looking forward to the treats and enjoying his new role as helper.

"You have changed a lot this year," I told Nathan. "How?" Nathan was not one to waste words.

"You act much older, and you show that you care about other people."

Nathan and I had struggled together toward this day. I learned to appreciate his free and cheerful spirit, and Nathan learned to listen, especially when I felt he was rough-housing in the church. We passed out the treats, and Nathan possessed a certain air of poise and authority. *Every minute we have with a child counts.*

Parents, grandparents, and teachers at church have limited time with each child. Some surveys indicate that parents often spend ten minutes or less a day with their children. Beyond trying to stretch those minutes, where can parents—themselves often stressed and overworked—whittle out the opportunities that a family needs to bond and grow together?

Nathan had a renewed image of himself to live up to, all from just a few minutes of conversation. An adult had noticed his new maturity; and with a child, that counts. *Whatever time we as parents, grandparents, or teachers spend with a child, whether at play or at home, every minute counts.*

We want to keep at least three things in mind:

1. How can I show this child that the world can be a very good place indeed, and that she or he has a role to play in God's creation?

2. How can I nurture relationships that are fun, positive, and hospitable, helping this child be inclusive and hopeful, even when the way becomes rocky?

3. What are the memory builders that will become a part of this child's life forever and will continue to draw him or her to God and to the church?

We have only to look at some of the children of the Bible to see that God does, indeed, have plans for every one of God's children.

Jeremiah was assured that God knew him even in the womb; the poet soul of David responded to the beauty of pastures and sheep at his childhood home. Jacob and Esau were competitive siblings who did not get along well but were reconciled in their adult years as they responded to God's will. Our children are no different.

As we share the stories of children in the Bible, we expand our children's motivation to be worshipful, helpful, and hopeful.

Part of our role in helping children discern their place in God's plan will be to recognize and encourage their strengths. Nathan is definitely "Mr. Personality." To know him is to grin in recognition of all the mischievous, creative, challenging, outgoing kids you ever knew. But helping him to avoid some of the pitfalls that await mischievous children is also part of what we do as parents and teachers.

We gotta have patience. *Every minute counts.* There is little benefit to be derived from scolding or unusual punishment. Guiding his energy into other channels will work better with Nathan, especially if we help him identify and claim his accomplishment.

Nurturing good relationships with others in the family or in the classroom is a skill that has to be developed for most of us. We are likely to advise our youngsters, "Be good" or "Play nice." Just what does that mean anyway? Must a child swallow anger at injustice, or is there a way to negotiate peace?

✳✳✳✳✳✳✳✳✳✳✳✳✳✳✳✳✳✳✳✳✳✳✳✳✳✳✳✳✳

Our granddaughter, she of the lovely blue eyes, had her name written on the chalkboard for talking during silent time. When her teacher told us about it, she said, "I knew immediately that I had made a mistake. I received a long, reproachful blue gaze from that little girl." Emily had not been talking; and although the teacher acknowledged the mistake, she never apologized to the child. Emily loved that teacher and still does, but it was not a good example of justice for a little girl who had been misjudged.

Children are very concerned about being fair, and every relationship must include justice whether or not it includes affection. In our family, we try to avoid any occasions that might induce Emily's blue gaze.

On long walks or car rides with children, introduce comments and questions about family relationships in the Bible. What about the parents of Jacob and Esau? Could it be that the controversies between the twin brothers were stimulated by favoritism? What about Moses: brought up as a privileged prince, yet bringing up his own children in the grim desolation of the desert. Do you think they ever resented God's mandate for their father? It might be easier for children to solve their own sibling problems after discussing some of the very issues that affected the children of the Bible.

As parents, let us be big on happy memories. Think back to your own happy memories. What now sustains you in adulthood? What makes you and your siblings laugh together now that you are grown? When were the moments you felt most loved, most valued as a family member?

I remember modest picnics at Island Park. It was not an island, and it really was not much of a park; but it did have two cages of animals—one of monkeys and one of raccoons. My handsome father loved those animals and could stand with his little girls for an hour watching their antics. He especially enjoyed the raccoons and chuckled when they washed their food in their water pans. Today we catch a lot of raccoons in our live traps, taking them far from the farm grain bins to live a happy life by the lake where we doubt if they wash their food. But just seeing these four-legged bandits helps me relive some of the happier days of childhood during the Great Depression and helps me remember that adults and children may remain bonded for decades by happy moments spent together.

* *

The "Nathans" in our lives will always be both a joy and a challenge to parents. We know that they are wonderfully and fearfully made, and that God, in God's creative wisdom, has a plan for these children as well. We cannot always discern the plan, but we love these children and offer prayerful guidance for their maturity in Christ. *Every minute we spend with our children counts.*

Questions for Discussion and Meditation

1. When I was a very young child, our pastor came out of his study and played games with us at vacation Bible school one day. The church lawn was full of big kids playing ball, but the pastor played our little-kid games with US. That is big on my list of happy memories! What early worship or Sunday school events do you remember that made an impression on you as a child?

2. If indeed *every minute counts,* what about the dreadful minutes when a parent loses his or her temper or makes accusations that are incorrect, nurtures expectations that are not realistic, quarrels with the neighbors? How do we explain and discuss those unholy moments with our children?

3. The older children in a family often have a big influence on the younger ones. How much responsibility should the older ones have to *make every minute count?* How are privileges granted in families with several children? What activities serve to bond families? How can the church help?

WILL OUR CHILDREN CARE?
BIBLE READING: 1 JOHN 4:11-12

In a world that sometimes seems utterly confusing, we wonder how we can possibly teach our children to care about one another. Is caring taught or caught?

- A nine-year-old jumps into the pool at a birthday party and pulls out a younger boy who is struggling in deep water. He holds the boy's head above water until a parent comes to help.

- Two children are injured in a car accident. As the mother lies helpless, the five-year-old extracts his younger brother from the child carseat and takes him to safety in a nearby cabin.

- A four-year-old runs joyfully through the meadow. She stops, returns to her grandmother, and takes her hand. "Let me help you, Grandma," she says. "It might be hard to walk here."

Whether children show caring and kindness in the everyday business of life or in the emergencies, most of them react according to their own experience. The best way parents teach their children to be caring individuals is to show caring daily for each other and for their family.

RESPOND AND RESPECT

Take time to respond to a child's concern, even though it does not seem so dire to you. A little girl called her grandmother in tears. "I took my new birthday dolly to the babysitter's, and the dog chewed her arm off."

"Oh, dear," said her grandmother, "you had better bring her to the hospital at my house."

When the little girl arrived, Grandmother had already assembled cushions and shoeboxes—a veritable hospital ward. She had a make-believe stethoscope and a multitude of bandages. The little girl put on a nurse's cap; and together she and Doctor Grandma attended to the dolly, as well as to an interesting array of stuffed animals.

At last the little girl retired to her rocking chair, holding the injured but recovering doll. "I think," she said, "that when you take your dolly to the Grandma Hospital, it is the best day in the whole world."

We cannot always respond through actual deeds; even parents cannot create miracles! But we must respond appropriately to every need, every question, every circumstance. No child should be ignored, even if the response is that you need some quiet time right now but will deal with it later. Such responses show respect for the individual and teach the child to show respect to others and to care for them as well.

MODEL AND MENTOR

It is not easy to be a role model! Yet we can expect to be nothing less for our children. I am thankful to have had a mother who always treated others with thoughtful concern. She was a teacher in a one-room country school, and one year her school board bought ice cream for the end-of-school picnic. Now, these were Depression days, and ice cream was a rare treat. Miracle of miracles, there was some left over; and the school board generously told Mom to take it home to her family.

All the way home I thought about that ice cream. Wow, ice cream for supper! However, as Mom began to muse about the children on the next farm, who probably had not had ice cream for weeks, I began to see the handwriting on the wall. This was not to be our ice cream. My sister and I put that ice cream freezer in our little red wagon and dragged it down the road to the neighbors. Never will I forget the delight of those children nor the flush of pleasure on their mother's face as she scooped carefully measured bowls of ice cream for all of us.

> ### *We don't need to preach caring and sharing; we just need to do it.*

Although parents are not usually thought of as mentors, we share some of the characteristics of mentors. The character of Mentor in Greek mythology gave wise advice and shared knowledge with his friend's son. As parents, we intend that our advice will be wise and that our children will follow it. Although there are family rules, there are also moments when advice is given and choices are possible. A mentor does not force; a mentor offers friendship and loving support; a mentor teaches and guides. Mentors personify caring attitudes and fair judgment. In the heat of the moment, I have known parents to forget this!

COMPARE AND CREATE

Consequences are a great teacher. Point out positive consequences much more often than the negative, although sometimes that is certainly necessary, too.

- It was a good idea for you to shovel Mrs. Brown's walk. How badly we would have felt if she had fallen on the ice!

- I did not realize the dog's water dish needed to be scoured out. We would not want him to drink dirty water and get sick. Thank you.

- How nice that you cleaned the kitchen for me! When I feel better, it will be a real pleasure to fix our meals.

- I am glad you told your teacher that you missed her while she was gone. Everyone likes to know he or she is doing a good job.

It is not so hard, is it? Children do so many little things that we can appreciate and encourage.

Perhaps most important of all, we try to create an environment where caring for others is the norm. Jesus "went about doing good" (Acts 10:38b), teaching and showing us ways to be more caring. We encourage those instincts in our children as we create opportunities for them to share, when we lead in intercessory prayer, when we rejoice over the achievements and blessings of others, when we respect and respond to their needs, when we model kind behavior as we mentor, and when we create places of quiet peace and security in our homes. God bless us, everyone!

Questions for Discussion and Meditation

1. Spending time and showing love even in small amounts makes "the best day in the whole world" for children. What are the best days in the whole world for you personally? When do you make someone else's day the best day in the whole world? When is God's care most felt in your family relationships?

2. How does your congregation express its love for others outside your fellowship? How do you express your caring for the lonely? the bereaved? the incapacitated? It is not only the poor who need our loving care. Name others to whom your church can show loving concern. How will you do this? What effect might this have on your children?

3. Are you a mentor in either a formal or an informal relationship? Share some of your experiences, though never any that are confidential. Would there be value in your congregation engaging in a formal mentoring program whereby mentors receive training and support? Investigate how this might be done.

COME, YE THANKFUL CHILDREN
BIBLE READING: PSALM 95:1-7

"Kids expect too much. They think they are entitled to every gadget on the market," said a grumpy and somewhat wistful grandfather.

There's that word again. *Entitlement* was not even in the dictionary a few decades ago, yet today many are concerned about the double concept and what it will mean in the future for their families and for our culture itself. What are the legitimate expectations for children, and how may we encourage youngsters to be appreciative of their blessings?

> *When is entitlement real, and when is it a presumptuous expectation?*

Certainly we want adequate shelter, nutritious food, education, and love for every child. We abhor violence, abuse, and poverty. We cherish opportunities to share the awesomeness of God and God's care for children. We know that some children take all these advantages for granted, giving no thought to the magnificence of God's love, to the efforts of parents to provide for them, nor to the agencies whose help they may occasionally require. In a time of a tight economy, many youngsters and youth have had to face an unexpected reduction in their wants and desires. The opulence of past decades no longer serves as the yardstick of expectations.

How can faithful families thank and praise God for what they have? In Bible times, the Israelites celebrated three great feasts at the Temple in Jerusalem. As the pilgrims climbed the hill to the Temple, they praised God with song, anthems, dancing, and instruments. Some of these Songs of Ascent are believed to be Psalms 120 to 134. Here we see that the people thanked God for the privilege of entering the Temple, for "things too great and too marvelous for me" (Psalm 131:1b), for family and kindred. Their joy in worship and praise is evident to us as we read these psalms many centuries later.

We, too, can set aside times when our families and our congregations recall with thanks and praise the holiness of our divine God and our thankfulness for the gift of Jesus. The American Thanksgiving Day is a special day on which we honor the Pilgrims and the early founders of our nation, thanking God for their accomplishments. This holiday, however, should not be the only time when we bow in remembrance and honor before God. Family and community structures may seek God's blessing and respond to God's guidance every day.

Rituals of thanksgiving are common in the Bible. Since most people did not read and write, the celebrations and rituals were a way of passing on and remembering past events and God's continual presence and care. We, too, can make rituals a part of our family's growth in awareness and appreciation.

On Memorial Day, ask family members to remember someone in the past who contributed to their lives in an important way. This can be someone from history, an armed services veteran, someone from your congregation who has passed away, someone precious in the family. Remember these people, and say a prayer of thankfulness.

On Independence Day, ask each member to lift up one thing about our country that is especially meaningful to them. In our family, this resulted in years of fascinating history study as we each tried to uncover and dazzle other family members with unknown facts. What thankful patriots we became!

On Thanksgiving Day, children may wish to thank God for a special food; on Christmas Day, for a special part of the Nativity that they love. The point is, on every special day, the family can think together of blessings and can form the habit of thankful prayer. In our family we still have a little trouble with Groundhog Day. Groundhogs to us mean holes in the pasture or runway, a dangerous nuisance; and none of us has yet to see a groundhog out on a cold day. But God must have made groundhogs for something or other, so we merely give thanks that we do not have to know everything.

I must admit, in our household, we sometimes spontaneously made up a holiday. In the spring, we might have "National Wild Gooseberry Day" or an "Annual Stick Pick-up Day" after an ice storm has damaged trees. Special activities and treats are added to a litany of thankfulness. Who would not be thankful for gooseberry pie or for a hot dog roast around a stick fire at sunset?

Children and adults alike need to be thankful in their relationships with others. Most of us teach our youngsters to thank Grandma and Aunt Nattie for their love and their presents; but it takes our example for children to realize that a thankful attitude may also include appreciation for the public librarian who checks out the books, the postal worker who faithfully delivers the mail, the person who invites us to a birthday party. Entitlement includes much more than "expecting something for nothing." We also need to avoid taking for granted the courteous and caring treatment that others offer. There are, of course, legitimate programs of entitlement where a contribution has been made and the recipient is due the reward. Be thankful for those, too!

As appreciative as we are for material comfort, it may be healthier for the whole world for us to get along with less. Examining our own excesses may lead us to sharing more with others or even to examining issues of justice. The happiest children are not the ones with the most stuff; they are the ones whose parents care and are thankful for the blessing of children in the home.

Questions for Discussion and Meditation

1. How do you explain to your child the difference between desires and needs? If it is difficult for you to provide what a child needs, where do you go for help? Do your neighbors support you or criticize you?

2. Most of us agree that children can have too much in the way of material gadgets. How much is enough? How can your children stay abreast of new technological developments if it is impossible to have personal cell phones, computers, and games?

3. List five things for which you think your child is genuinely thankful. Compare your personal list with the child's. Talk about the differences. Is thankfulness a part of your family's value system? Why or why not?

4. It is difficult to be thankful when your family is in need, or when you are worried about the future. How will you share with your children that God is always with us, even in times of poverty and need?

WHEN HISTORY IS NOT A MYSTERY
BIBLE READING: DEUTERONOMY 31:10-13

One branch of our family would probably be very rich if it were not for the pirates. John Felkner and his sons had driven a herd of cattle all the way from the Midwest to California during the gold rush. Pocketing a substantial profit, they turned to sea transportation part of the way home. Unfortunately, a band of pirates came upon them off the coast of California and confiscated all their money, and the Felkners returned home poorer than when they started.

When they heard this story, our children suddenly became very interested in the gold rush, cattle drives across the West, and particularly in the pirates who prowled the coast of California. Nineteenth-century American history was not a set of dates to them, it was the adventures and mysteries of the people who lived in that time; and our children wanted to claim a piece of the action. They played pirates in the backyard, sailed for Africa in the plastic wading pool, and spent hours trying to herd the black Angus cattle in our pastures. *History does not have to be a mystery!*

Can you image the stories that Methuselah must have told his children, his grandchildren, maybe even his great-great-great grandchildren? After all, Methuselah lived to be 969 years old, so he had probably seen almost everything his part of the world had to offer.

Or what about Moses, brought up to be a prince, then becoming a homeless shepherd who had to depend upon his father-in-law for a good job? The Bible is an intriguing book, full of thousands of wonderful history stories. These were written down after many years in the hope that the history of humankind's relationship to God would somehow guide the generations still to be born.

Family histories are intriguing and most often reveal national or community history as well. Part of our community history claims that an old Native American Indian burial ground was used by Mormons who suffered a flu epidemic while passing through. Inquiry at Salt Lake City revealed no trail passed this burial ground. Years later, a local historian traced the Waubonsie Trail, and, sure enough, the modern highway had curved away from the trail that at one time included this cemetery. Some groups of Mormons had indeed evidently used the Waubonsie Trail and had buried their dead in the Indian burial ground.

> *Family histories are intriguing and most often reveal national or community history as well.*

School children interested in this story found that some of their families had come to America in the surge of Mormon immigration from Europe. Others found letters that their grandmothers cherished, written from the "old country" to their hardy relatives in America. This extracurricular interest in history gave them a greater feel for the settlement of our land than any memorization of dates or battles.

My own interest in a lesser-known nation of Native Americans from Ohio and Michigan, the Wyandots, was stimulated by their relationship to the first Methodist mission project in our country. The story of their removal to Oklahoma in the nineteenth century led to an interest in the other Native American nations close to them. My study of Chief Tarhe led me to an appreciation of other great diplomats who were Native Americans. Telling these stories to children dramatically changed their Western movie concepts of the Native American Indian. When we eat sweet corn, we think of the ones who first grew it; when we see wild chicory along the road, we marvel at the ingenuity of the Fox and Sac who ground the roots for a sort-of coffee beverage. When we travel, we identify the many native words used to name the cities and towns of our nation. History overcomes mystery, and we are eager to pursue it!

Churches have history, too. A stained-glass window in a small country church at Jerome, Iowa, commemorates the individual who came on an Orphan Trail out of the eastern part of our nation. Another church split into two congregations over a bushel of apples. The man who traditionally had provided a bushel of apples for the children in the Christmas program was chagrined when another individual usurped his gift with better apples. He departed to establish another congregation down the street.

What awesome stories there are to savor, whether they be family, national, or church stories. The creative parent uses stories as a teaching tool, just as Jesus did. History does not have to be a mystery. Instead, it can become the means through which we learn and grow to appreciate and even improve our society.

> *History does not have to be a mystery. Instead, it can become the means through which we learn and grow to appreciate and even improve our society.*

Though we would not wish to burden children unduly, and certainly we would not wish to frighten them, we can encourage their awareness of history in the making. After all, children are really voters in training. Some of their concepts of both past and present are developed by the culture and society in which they live. Converse freely with your children. Ask them what issues are in the news from the city council? Today, the mayor of our town appealed to the residents to look at every intersection where children might be crossing on their way to school to see if there are bushes, trees, or other impediments, which might blind car drivers as they approach the intersection. I urged children from my Sunday school class (tweens) to make this survey and report it to the mayor.

What about state issues? Our state has established new no-smoking areas by law. Is this fair? Why or why not? When is it okay for government to place restrictions on its citizens? Elementary kids might enjoy this one. Listen to all sides, follow developments in the news, assure children that this is history, and they are a part of it.

And, of course, always keep the issues of peacekeeping before children. Memorizing the dates of wars and battles is not so much use for character information. Knowing the stories of Ethan Allen, Harriet Tubman, John F. Kennedy, and probably their own grandfathers and grandmothers will make the lessons of history strike home. A famous historian once said, "Those who do not know the lessons of history are doomed to repeat them."

We are always aware that the Bible is the story of a people and their relationship to God. Stories told around the campfires of the early Israelite people, sometimes written down centuries later, are the history stories that teach us of God. *History is never a mystery if we take its lessons to heart and use them to grow closer to our Creator and to Jesus the Christ.*

Questions for Discussion and Meditation

1. What stories of your early family would you share with your children? Are these warning stories or positive stories?

2. Who established the church to which you belong? Why did they feel the need for a church in this place?

3. Name a Bible story that has especially enriched your life or the life of your family. Who wrote the book? Why do you think it was included in the canon? Was the protagonist of this story a hero who could be a role model or a rascal from whom your children could absorb a lesson? Or both?

PART TWO
WINTER
FALLING SNOW

THE POTATO PEELER GUY
BIBLE READING: 1 CORINTHIANS 10:24

There are probably not many churches that have gratefully accepted a potato peeler for the church kitchen as an appropriate memorial gift. There was a dedicated farmer in our church who asked to be put on the Mission Committee. "I want to be where the action is," he grinned. From then on, the Potato Peeler Guy appeared in the church kitchen before every Mission Committee dinner, leaving his fields and his harvest in order to peel that night's buckets of potatoes. When he died, the Mission Committee gave a cow to Heifer Project and a potato peeler to the church kitchen in memory of this good farmer and his many contributions to our church. There was no job too small for the Potato Peeler Guy, from peeling potatoes to repairing the roof. His mission was to lend a hand.

> *We teach our children to be concerned about the welfare of their neighbors, doing so because that is God's will.*

We understand that the faith formation of a child is often stimulated by the adults who are a part of his life. Humility is not an asset we see too often; we are more likely to be impressed by persons of wealth or position than we are with those among us who seek the good of their neighbors first. We teach our children to be concerned about the welfare of their neighbors, doing so because that is God's will. God surely intends as well that every child shall experience self-awareness as a child of God. It follows that an individual with such confident self-knowledge will find no honest task too humble, no opportunity to do good in Jesus' name to be without merit, even a boring job like peeling potatoes!

Sometimes the most mischievous children are those without the knowledge of a loving God. Indeed, children grow toward more positive self-awareness and a desire to help others as they observe the caring Christian adults around them. Obviously, the first thing we must do as the parents, relatives, or simply as the neighbors of children is to give them positive attention.

- One man teaches his grandson and any friends he has in tow to work on cars. These kids know how to change the oil! They are learning about the intricacies of an engine's insides.
- Through a special government program, deer that are harvested from farms or city suburbs with the proper hunting tags may be commercially processed and distributed to the poor. But who knows how to cook deer? One hunter offers a class on how to prepare wild game. Whole families come to church to learn the technique, then feast on a good meal.
- A widow offered her garage as a place for kids to work on their bikes, provided they are supervised and the doors remain open while the kids are there. Tools are provided. There have been a few losses, but most of the time the other kids know where the tools might be and repossess them for the Bike Site.

Self-awareness and respect for others go hand in hand when children are able to acknowledge shortcomings and helped to overcome them. I used a gaming technique to help a "tattler" to realize that his persistent attitude of righteousness and blame was becoming really annoying to the rest of us. We drew a complicated trail on a piece of posterboard, with squares marked from beginning to end. Using markers and a die, the players traversed the trail, hoping, of course, to land on squares such as: *You helped a neighbor in the garden. Go ahead three spaces.* Occasionally, however, the squares were not so positive: *You told on your brother instead of helping him clean up the mess he made. Go back five spaces.* I left plenty of blank spaces so that the children could make up both Good Deeds and Bad Deeds. Several of them unloaded about the tattling; the point was made with minimum discomfort. Later, we talked about Joseph in the Bible, who tattled on his brothers, earning only scorn and enmity. God continued to love Joseph; and God continues to love us, especially when we seek to correct our shortcomings and to be thoughtful of our family and neighbors.

A hermit moved into a shack a couple miles from our home. While most of the neighbors ignored him, and some even tormented him, my dad walked to the shack to get acquainted. He discovered that the man was a Russian immigrant. (In later years, we had to wonder how this man managed to leave Russia at that particular time in history.) This new neighbor was not yet comfortable with the English language nor with American ways. Dad, himself an immigrant twenty-five years earlier, respected the hermit's desire for privacy; he offered his friendship and help. They got along fine, and Dad put an end to the heckling done by neighborhood teenagers. The lesson was not lost on any of us. Loving our neighbor as ourselves was a far stretch, but Dad made it seem natural.

Neighboring in its purest sense is simply the extension of God's love to others. The good Samaritan, though his people were despised by the Jews, found a helpless Jewish merchant beside the road and cared for him. We can discuss with our children the "helpless merchants" of our time and decide appropriate ways to be neighborly. What about immigrants, both legal and illegal? Should we be neighbors to both? What neighborliness is helpful and appropriate for each? What would Jesus do?

Serving God is always the path to true happiness, and we serve God best when we are cognizant of the needs of others and strive to be helpful. Whether befriending the hermit or peeling the potatoes, the good guys are those who put God and their neighbors first.

Questions for Discussion and Meditation

1. What injustices might Jesus see in your neighborhood or your community? What might Jesus expect you to do about it?

2. Do people see the Christ in you and/or your family members? You probably do not cause the lame to walk or the blind to see. What can you do?

3. Who does the humble tasks when your congregation sponsors a public dinner? Are children encouraged to help?

4. What holy habits does your family practice? What other holy habits could you practice? Do your children help choose holy habits for the family?

WALKING HUMBLY WITH GOD
BIBLE READING: MICAH 6:8

The second-graders at Central School were among the most enthusiastic fans of our high school basketball team. It had been a winning season, and the town was full of high hopes for a state tournament. Those basketball players were heroes to the second-grade boys; and when one boy was promised a birthday party, he immediately sent invitations to the whole high school basketball team. His parents warned him that his high school heroes were not likely to have the time for a second-grade party, but he remained hopeful.

You got it. Two of those high school boys arrived for the party. They played games, shot baskets in the backyard, and sang the birthday song before eating cake with their second-grade friends. Never was there a more successful party!

- Walking humbly with God involves a faith that worships and honors God in all things, relying on God's guidance and answering God's call in a humble, obedient manner.

- Walking humbly with God can happen in small, everyday ways.

Those teenagers were not looking for immortal fame, though I expect that is what they will receive from the second-graders. They just thought it would be a blast to show up and demonstrate some team spirit to the children. Mission accomplished. A misplaced sense of importance or arrogance could have prevented the experience. When I asked the parents how they encouraged such a spirit of fun and equality in their teenagers, they said, "We try to teach our children to put God first, the family second, and our church and community third, before they think of self-interest. We all wanted the birthday boy to have a good party."

"Do justice, and to love kindness, and to walk humbly with your God" (Micah 6:8). What a high standard for anyone!

The justice part is not hard to understand, though it may be hard to practice. Most young children have fairly set ideas about being fair. Whether among siblings at home or within the school classroom or Sunday school class, they are quick to identify any hint of injustice. *Play fair* is the seminal rule of young lives. Parents who insist on equality; who identify and discuss cases of injustice in the evening news; who champion people for their worth in God's eyes, not their status in this world, are setting the tone and practice for justice in the character of their children. Sometimes self-interest must give way to justice.

Loving kindness is not too hard, either, so long as we give children the experiences of both receiving and extending kindness. At a time of grief for me, a kindergarten child brought me a cross made from a foam meat tray, on which she had pasted a sticker, "I am praying for you." How precious the kindness of a child! A kind spirit will extend to animals, both domestic and wild. We cannot be uncaring to our pets and the wildlife around us and still call ourselves kind individuals. One little girl brought her pet frog to our farm. She asked if we had a nice place for him, since he was getting too big for a glass jar. We released the frog in a pond near a culvert where he would be able to swim and catch lots of mosquitoes for supper. Occasionally, I send an e-mail to this little girl when I see frogs at that pond; we think probably he is the grandfather of a large family by now. Certainly, this is kinder than life in a glass jar!

Walking humbly with God is a harder task. The prophet Micah was protesting the false righteousness and the hypocrisy of those who professed to love and honor God, yet who were cheating others, being deceitful in their actions and attitudes. Micah was certain that their burning of sacrifices did no good unless they also cleansed their hearts and followed God's way, which was certainly the way of justice, kindness, and humility before the God we know.

Pride is perhaps the first thing we must root out of our lives if we, too, wish to walk humbly with our God. In a day when having the most, being the first, or possessing the best is a mark of success, it may be difficult for parents to stress humility. A teenager is scholastically exceptional as well as an accomplished, award-winning musician. I asked the modest, smiling young woman her secret. "My folks taught me that God gives us our gifts and talents. We did nothing to earn them. I am responsible for using my gifts in the best way. That's all there is to it."

Of course, we want to commend our children for good work; for positive attitudes; for efforts at cooperation, justice, and kindness. Elaborate and unjustified praise, however, may do more harm than good; and certainly comparing the achievements of youngsters with each other may result in feelings of superiority on one hand or of embarrassment and inferiority on the other.

- Accept each child as a gift from God, complete with talents or shortcomings.
- Encourage each child to be unique, able to polish skills or overcome problems.
- Explain that the whole world is connectional. Each chickadee, each opossum, each mountain or desert, each prairie or tree, each child or adult, each lonesome frog, all are created to be a part of God's universe. How special can that be!
- Our human task as we walk humbly with God is to live as Jesus taught us, loving God with all our hearts and our neighbors as ourselves. Surely justice and kindness will follow!

Questions for Discussion and Meditation

1. We have all heard that "pride goeth before a fall." Has this ever been true in your life? in the lives of your children? What has this to do with walking humbly with your God?

2. In our competitive society, children often vie for position and recognition. How does your church and your family encourage cooperation over competition?

3. How important is self-esteem in the lives of children? What is the relationship between self-esteem and humility? What are the marks of an individual who walks humbly with God?

KINGDOM LIVING
BIBLE READING: LUKE 17:20-21

A dove browsed for seed under my birdfeeders. All was peaceful until a Brewer's blackbird challenged her right to the spilled seed. Immediately, she turned toward him, getting in a quick peck before the befuddled blackbird retreated. A boat-tailed grackle took his chance next, and again the dove drove him off with dispatch.

What is going on here? Isn't the dove destined to be the symbol of peace? She is certainly keeping peace on my west lawn today. Her very presence has silenced the raucous birds that have been scolding from my maple tree. Even a squirrel turns his head from his ear of corn to keep an eye on Mrs. Dove.

We wonder if nature can teach us anything about kingdom living. In the animal world where might makes right, we see some of our human characteristics. Mrs. Dove is feeding nestlings; obviously, she needs that seed to stay strong herself. After a few seeds, Mrs. Dove carries some of the treasure back to her young, returning again and again for a refill. Every new mother understands the need to stay energetic and to feed and protect her young. Mrs. Dove is not exactly peaceful as she carries forward those natural instincts. She will pass this behavior on to her young: peace when possible, survival of the species in any case.

Kingdom living starts young.

We pass on those same values to our children. For humans, hopefully, the "survival of the species" will include compromise, meeting the needs of others, sharing, dialog, and empathy. We need to hone our peace skills, not by driving everyone else to our will, but by examples of peaceful and productive behavior in the home and community. Kingdom living starts young.

The Epistles of the New Testament are a constant source of advice as we strive to live as the recipients of God's grace. Paul, James, and others give us the facts, plain and true: God saves us through Jesus the Christ; and because we are saved (believing disciples), we desire to live a life of service and love. Simple as that. Kingdom living may be difficult for children as they struggle with issues of identity, dependence, self-care, or even competition for resources and attention. Kingdom living may take some effort at stressful times. Blessed is the parent who takes it seriously!

Hebrews 13:16 advises us, "Do not neglect to do good and to share what you have, for such sacrifices are pleasing to God." That is a good place to start with children. If they understand that "doing good" means sharing, helpfulness, obedience, honesty, and fairness, with the many deeds that illustrate these virtues, "doing good" becomes a joy and a natural part of their lives.

A seven-year-old neighbor delights in doing crafts with her talented but physically challenged grandmother. We in the neighborhood are often the recipients of her latest skills: a tiny Christmas manger made from a walnut shell, small angels from foam and lace, a decorated ring from the plastic pull on a milk container, an Easter cross from craft sticks. Her gifts are received with appreciation and love, even sometimes with cookies. Hannah goes about doing good and brightening every day. She knows all about kingdom living.

Doing good includes good manners and respect for others. Many children are not comfortable with the elderly or with those who are physically challenged or disabled. Roleplay these encounters with children. Teach them how to approach the elderly at family or social gatherings. In my childhood, the tradition in our Danish church taught that the younger ones always approached the older ones with their greetings, a practice I still find charming though not so frequently encountered. Sunday school classes or other groups that visit nursing homes may be taught a few questions or conversation openers to use as they learn to know and appreciate the elderly.

A group of youngsters from a small church asked to give a tea party at a nursing home. What fun we had! The boy who poured tea had never been to such a party; but he rose to the occasion as other children pushed wheelchairs to the tea table, passed cookies, and conversed with the residents. One elderly lady said, "I never went to a better party in my life!"

Physically challenged persons especially love their relationships with children. The newer custom of streamlining challenged children in the school system has, I think, added to the understanding and comfort of all groups of youngsters. Curiosity and shyness give way to friendly greetings and helpfulness. I once watched a group of fourth-grade girls at a swim party with their challenged friend. That whole evening, she was never alone; the other girls simply and unobtrusively passed around the responsibility of seeing that the challenged youngster was safe in the water the whole time. Such impressive learning will be carried into adulthood to enrich the lives of everyone.

Modern technology does not particularly encourage these behaviors. Television, movies, websites, and blogs offer choices; however, those decisions must be made by the parents during the early formative years of the child.

Our own kingdom living is always under survey. In this as in everything else, our example teaches the young. We cannot expect children to behave in ways we have not demonstrated ourselves. *Kingdom living may need to be explained: We are trying always to live as Jesus lived and taught.* It is sometimes difficult, and we often need to be forgiven and guided in new ways, adults as well as children. This includes our use of language. Words that offend have no place in a caring community and, in fact, may prevent our children from employing new and more appropriate vocabularies.

Even so small a thing impacts our kingdom living. If we put a name to it, children are more likely to identify themselves as children of the Kingdom and to accept the joy of kingdom living.

Questions for Discussion and Meditation

1. How does your congregation relate to the physically challenged? Is there a wheelchair available? earphones for the hard of hearing? parking services? How do children help?

2. Is there a congregational or community center for the mentally challenged? a respite provided for caretakers?

3. What evidence would a stranger see that your household is engaged in kingdom living? What personal changes do we need to make? What does it mean that the kingdom of God is within you?

RAISING GENEROUS CHILDREN IN A GREEDY SOCIETY
BIBLE READING: MATTHEW 6:19-21

On my fireplace mantle are three precious possessions: a Charlie Brown doll, a stuffed moose toy, and a little dancing bear. These were gifts from my great-grandchildren when their mother suggested that they give something of themselves to me for my birthday. What better way than to share a beloved toy! Of course, I must remember to be generous in turn, so we will play together with these toys when they visit.

Raising generous children does not just happen. We live in a greedy society in which having more, consuming more, and wanting more are part of daily life, even for children. Bombarded by television commercials—competition for more toys, more treats, and more privileges—children are apt not to value generosity unless they are the recipients of it. Generosity is a fruit of the spirit; and children who know Jesus are most apt to exhibit the values that Jesus embraced, lived, and taught.

As we all know, being an example is the best way to teach—good or bad. So we begin with ourselves and our attitudes as we consider this challenge. Teachers and parents urge children to share, probably several times a day. Our own sharing may be less visible, and we need to take a quick survey. Do we share our home by opening it for Girl Scout or 4-H meetings? Do we encourage the church choir by hosting an early Sunday morning breakfast? Do we send cupcakes for the whole class on the teacher's birthday? You can add dozens of ideas to this list. The important thing is that we need to involve our children in both the fun of planning and the fun of doing the generous acts that enrich our lives.

Generosity grows best in an environment of love and caring. Parents and guardians encourage more than material generosity. We realize that, though we live in a prosperous and greedy society, not everyone has what they need. If our children see that they indeed have more than enough and that there are those around them who do not have as much, then giving and generosity have added meaning. We do not have more because we are better; our having more imposes a new and sober responsibility. We share with God's other beloved ones in order that we may all enjoy these blessings of God.

High on the list of generous sharing is the gift of time. Whether this is a chat with a child in the aisles of the grocery store, a few moments pushing the swing at the park, extra outings for a Sunday school class, or taking an elderly friend to a movie, every sharing of time given cheerfully and happily is an example of generosity to our children. They, too, can be encouraged to be generous with their time: write a note to a distant grandparent, teach a younger child to toss a ball, help a teacher carry books to her car, chat awhile with one who is lonely. These are significant gifts in a society that is mainly in a rush. Generosity includes encouragement and positive reinforcement of the acts and accomplishments of others. Sadly, some of us are stingy with praise and well-wishing. This is not to suggest that we give artificial praise where it is not deserved, but a generous spirit will express joy when others have been blessed. I will always remember the favorite words of a dear friend, "You can do it!" she would exclaim. Whether our families were learning to water ski, attempting to score on the basketball court, trying to overcome a mighty knot in our lives, or experiencing financial difficulties, my friend always was there with the words, "You can do it! Come on, you can do it!" Her generous spirit encourages me years after her death.

Though we insist that children should help out with family chores simply because they are part of the family and benefit from its existence, still it is possible for children to earn money in special circumstances. I pay a grandson to clean out the rain gutters or paint the deck, but he does scores of other errands and chores for me with a grin on his face and ice cream bar in hand. Generosity works both ways!

Several children in a Sunday school class made bead bracelets and cross bookmarks for a freewill offering that paid for magnetic paint for their classroom. Now the spiritual task is to see if we can share our gain so that another class may also have a magnetic wall in their room.

To become more aware of the effect of generosity in a greedy world, make two simple charts for one week:

> Acts of Generosity We Did This Week
>
> Acts of Generosity We Received This Week

Encourage family members to compare charts, to thank one another for acts of generosity, and to ask how they can extend this spiritual practice beyond their homes.

A little girl on vacation with her parents stayed at a nice motel. How delighted she was when the maid left a wrapped candy on each pillow! The next time she and her parents helped out at the homeless shelter, this little girl spent her allowance for candy, which she carefully distributed to each bed at the shelter.

There is another whole world out there, crying for our help. A nation with only six percent of the world's population is using thirty percent of the world's resources. *We must bring to bear everything Jesus taught about generosity if we hope to heal the world. Only when we share our material goods, our time, our love, and our earnest care for all people will true generosity prevail in a greedy society.*

Question for Discussion and Meditation

How would you explain to children about storing up treasures in heaven? Since Paul declares that we are saved by faith alone, do these verses have any value to you, or are they among the "works" that are not saved? Why then does generosity matter to children, or to us?

THE STORY'S THE THING
BIBLE READING: DEUTERONOMY 11:18-23

Almost every family has a storyteller, an individual who seems to know the important family stories from generations back. These stories are not just family reunion entertainment; they are used to encourage, motivate, or even correct younger members of the family.

Case in point: For four generations, our family has been cautioned against gambling. Great Uncle Louie once sold his cattle the day the carnival came to town and by the next morning had lost all the profits in the carnival gambling tents. As a child, I was certainly impressed!

Stories of patience, strength, greed, courage, deceit, prejudice, love, and sacrifice can probably be found in most families. These stories—the good and the bad—give substance to our roots and encourage the development of wise family values.

Stories have long been instruments for instruction and faith formation. The stories of the patriarchs came to us from the oral tradition, as the early people of God recounted their history and their relationships with God around the campfire.

Jesus, the Master Storyteller, often used storytelling to get his point across. The parable of the good Samaritan teaches us about inclusiveness; after all, it was the outcast Samaritan who rescued the traveler, not the ones in the mainstream of religious life who might have been expected to show compassion. We learn forgiveness from the parable of the forgiving father and his prodigal son; we understand the seeking nature of God in the parable of the woman who repeatedly swept her house in search of the lost coin. Jesus taught by using the common experiences of life, weaving them into unforgettable stories that we call *parables*.

My friend Dana used Bible stories as positive reinforcement for her children. You told a bully to leave a little kid alone? You are as courageous as David! You collected sixteen cans of fruit for the homeless shelter? You remind me of Dorcas, who helped others. You are a reading partner with a younger child in your school? I remember that Jesus also welcomed and loved children.

Most young people enjoy the stories of their parents' lives. Though we are tempted to relate only the triumphs, we must also share some times of questionable judgment and what we learned from those experiences. I once went canoeing at midnight on the Cedar River in Iowa, a treacherous adventure at best. (My sister told on me and maintained for years that the telling was an act of nobility.) To this day, we use that story to discourage spontaneous and thoughtless risk-taking as well as to acknowledge that sometimes "telling" is an act of love.

One of the earliest ways we bond with our children is through cuddling, singing, and telling stories. I carried our children, wrapped in blankets, outside to see the full moon shining on drifts of snow. Stories of our ancestor who walked across the frozen Baltic Sea to reach his island home for the birth of a baby fill us with wonder at his courage. Thus, as parents, we express our own wisdom of God. We hand down a rich heritage when we share the stories that nourish our lives and our faith.

Questions for Discussion and Meditation

1. What sense of continuity or identity do family stories bring to you? Why would this be important?

2. For what purpose did the early Israelites treasure their oral tradition?

Going on to Perfection
Bible Reading: Romans 12:9-21

Two small boys in my neighborhood, ages five and six, returned home scratched, scuffed, and supremely happy. Their suspicious father asked, "Have you boys been fighting someone again?" Rules in that household held that the boys could defend themselves, but they were never to start a fight with other children. After admitting to the fight and receiving further parental words about their behavior, the five-year-old asked, "But Dad, if their dad says they can't start it, and you say we can't start it, who's going to start it?"

Sometimes it is really hard to give up our sins. Giving up a good scruff in the neighborhood seemed unreasonable to these little guys. Like most of us, they would like to hold onto some enjoyable moments, right or wrong. Let everyone else be like Jesus!

Jesus in the Temple was able to converse with and even teach the wise men because he was at one with God. Jesus, the perfect revelation of God, teaches, heals, guides, and saves out of the great love he has for all of humankind. We return that love when we know Jesus and strive to live our lives according to his Word. A beloved song puts it best: "I have decided to follow Jesus, no turning back, no turning back."

The question becomes, How can we as parents and teachers help our children "grow into perfection" (Hebrews 6:1), to understand the nature of God and the image of Jesus?

Going on to perfection is not a smooth journey, as any Christian will testify. We live in a world of clamorous temptation and questionable morality. Our responsibilities as parents and teachers are becoming ever more challenging as we seek to guide children.

I asked the children in my Sunday school class when they had felt closest to God. Their answers included: "When our church went Christmas caroling"; "When my niece was baptized, and the pastor let me hold the cup of water"; "When I had to go to the hospital, and my dad prayed for me"; "When I play the piano"; "When my dog wagged his tail and ate again after he had been hurt."

This provides an insight: Children who participate in the ministry and rituals of the church with their families grow in at-oneness with God. Age-inclusive activities, worship, and ministry nurture children spiritually as they experience God's presence with mature Christians. It is as important for us to nurture children spiritually as it is to provide opportunities for physical and intellectual growth.

But what about the children of non-churched families? Beth was such a child, living with her grandmother in a little house behind the church in a small town. Beth ran away from home almost every Sunday morning, making her way through the adjoining yards to arrive at the church for Sunday school and worship. Sometimes her hair was uncombed, or Beth came wearing her pajama top. Beth loved the singing, the Bible stories, her teachers; and everyone at church loved Beth. Her joyful smile energized us. Sunday was never really complete unless Beth ran away from home! (Yes, we told her grandmother where she was.) Today, several years later, Beth and her whole family attend church. Beth is a teacher of challenged children, where no doubt her smile lights up the classroom. The love, acceptance, and encouragement of Christian neighbors witnessed to the love of Jesus for a whole family who have since brought immeasurable warmth to our congregation.

Adults do not always feel the presence of God in their lives in the same way, and neither do children. A walk across timbered hills, a perch high in the maple tree, a silent ski across the falling snow, a particular piece of music, the wag of a dog's tail—all these speak of God. We cannot expect children to exhibit mature faith until they have first experienced God's presence in their hearts. But faith is faith, and we cannot limit the ways in which God calls our children. Experienced faith is a first step in the journey toward perfection. Heartfelt thankfulness for the wag of a dog's tail included!

Going on to perfection includes development of the qualities of courtesy, compassion, gentleness, kindness, reverence, love, humility, meekness, and patience. The apostle Paul can go on and on. We encourage such character traits by example and by quiet words of appreciation. As we decide to follow Jesus and to become more like him, both parents and their children grow in those ways. "No turning back, no turning back!"

Question for Discussion and Meditation

How is your family doing with courtesy, compassion, gentleness, kindness, reverence, love, humility, meekness, and patience? How will you know when (if) you reach perfection?

BLESSED ARE THE CHILDREN
BIBLE READING: MATTHEW 5:8

My friend Dorothy remembers going to Sunday school in a small rural church as a little girl. Her class sat around a table in the basement, where their teacher taught them a Bible verse every Sunday. Dorothy is now almost 80; but she says, "I still remember the Bible verses I learned, and they have given direction to my life."

We realize that not every child memorizes easily. Still, every child should have some basic knowledge of favorite Christian verses. Bible verses learned in childhood are likely to stay with us, even in cases of Alzheimer's or other disabilities of old age. Certainly, we want to be sure our children know the meaning of the Bible verses we ask them to memorize. Mere rote is not enough.

How blessed is the child whose parents are patient! The "blessing" verses of the New Testament are among the most cherished words of Jesus, and the patient parent will want to explain and memorize those Bible verses with their children. Still, most of us are not particularly eager to be poor or meek, and certainly not to mourn or be hungry and thirsty. Just what did Jesus have in mind?

Jesus' words in the Beatitudes are eschatological in nature; in other words, these Bible verses refer to the future kingdom of God. Just think of the impact! The poor will be blessed in the coming kingdom, the mournful will be comforted and cheered, mercy will be shown to those who have been merciful to others.

These blessings are not to be taken lightly but are promises that will be fulfilled in heaven. When explaining the Beatitudes to children, it might be helpful to use the word *because* instead of *for*. Most children are aware that consequences, either good or bad, happen *because* of preceding circumstances, actions, or attitudes.

Do not make memorization of Bible verses a chore. A mother once told me, "My children avoid reading the Bible. When they were younger, our church sent children to camp free if they would memorize many Bible verses. As their parents, we couldn't afford to pay for camp ourselves, so we insisted that our children spend their evenings learning Bible verses. It was a big mistake." I think of these children every time I drive past that church and its well-meaning congregation.

Nevertheless, Bible verses learned eagerly, perhaps through games or music, can remain with us and offer help in the most awful circumstances. One young man, a prisoner of war for six long years during the Vietnam War, told his family, "I remembered the Bible verses in prison, and they brought great comfort to me. I also knew my family members at home were reading and thinking about the Bible, and this gave me a feeling of connection with them. I cherished every word I could remember."

Memorization, particularly of the Beatitudes, can be fun. Try this: On separate slips of paper, write the first part of each Beatitude. The second part is written on other slips of paper, which are hidden around the room. Children draw a slip from the first group, then search for the second part. When each one is discovered, the children race back to secure another slip until all the Beatitudes have been assembled. Children check for accuracy in their Bibles. Play this game a few times for a couple of weeks, and the children will soon know every Beatitude. This is a cooperative game, not a competitive effort to "get the most." Perhaps at the end of the game, each child can have a small piece of candy, reminding them that in early Jewish times, the rabbi smeared honey on the slate of each new student. The student was urged to lick the honey off the slate to remember that learning is sweet. It still is.

When memorizing the Beatitudes with children, you will probably need to define some of the words. "Poor in spirit" means humble, without arrogance; "meek" means gentle, not warlike. The "pure in heart" are those who worship God alone, whose hearts are attuned to the holy. "Peacemakers" are those who long and act to achieve reconciliation with God and with humankind.

Most children memorize the Lord's Prayer from repeating it often in worship. However, you may want to review the prayer by printing each phrase on a narrow strip of posterboard. Mix up the phrases or scatter the phrases to different rooms of your house. Urge children to put the prayer in correct order. Explain word meanings. "Hallowed" means holy; "daily bread" means our food; "trespasses" or "debts" means sins. The prayer takes on added meaning for children with body movement or sign language, especially when done to music, and especially when done with their parents.

Children are the blessing of the future. Happy is the family that cherishes Scripture and builds its future upon the blessings of God's Word.

Questions for Discussion and Meditation

1. We are not saying that children are absolutely "pure in heart." What interpretation of this Bible verse will you share with your children?

2. What are some child-like characteristics that you believe God loves and that parents value?

To Touch the Heart of a Child
Bible Reading: 2 Corinthians 9:6-7

During Advent, many of our children take caps and mittens to the church Christmas tree to be given to needy children. Our choirs assemble at the nursing homes to sing for seniors. We bake cookies for the Christmas party at school. Trouble is, sometimes these activities do not extend into the rest of the year. Children whose hearts may be touched by the needs of the homeless, the hungry, and the lonely during the Christmas season might have neither the opportunity nor the inspiration to be in loving mission the rest of the year.

To care for others, to be sensitive to the needs of others, is surely among the first marks of a Christian. We have only to look at the example of Jesus to know that we serve God best when we touch the lives of others with care, acceptance, understanding, sympathy, and love. During Advent and Christmas, our hearts are stirred in a very special way; but how can we open opportunities for our children to embrace the experience of caring and to express this openly each day of the year?

A small boy walked with me in the mall. When we met a man on crutches, my little friend was both gleeful and wistful. "I wish I had a pair," he said. When we returned home, I dug out a pair of crutches Grandpa had used. Adjusting them to accommodate his small frame, I suggested that he walk on crutches until his mother came for him. An hour later a very tired little boy had had enough. "That's hard!" he exclaimed.

"The man at the mall must have been very tired, too," I said. "What can we do to help people who have to walk with crutches all the time?"

We decided we could open doors for people on crutches or in wheelchairs. We could be polite and allow them to get on the elevator first. We could offer to carry things. We believed that it was not enough to feel sorry that the man had to use crutches; we needed to act when our hearts are touched, just as Jesus did.

Safety must always concern us when children are involved. How well I remember the day when our friendly little daughter answered the door and led a man who was homeless into our living room. Fortunately, I stepped into the room at that moment and suggested that he wait under a shade tree while we made him a sandwich and a cup of coffee. Our little girl was touched by his situation. Our small town did not have a homeless shelter, but we were able to trace how local authorities helped people who were homeless and to make a donation to help buy meals for those who came into town. Later, we talked about how there were people who were homeless or hungry whom Jesus helped.

Some school districts mainstream youngsters in special education programs or offer a combination of educational opportunities. One child who is mentally challenged has the most delightful personality. She is a member of a class that has been together for several years; and although she has her special teacher and companion who goes to school with her, she has daily interaction with her classmates. She is involved in birthday parties, and she sings in a chorus. She loves to tease and laugh at jokes. This well-mannered and loved child has stimulated feelings of acceptance, helpfulness, and understanding in others. Children who may otherwise have overlooked or even laughed at those with mentally challenging conditions now feel empathy.

Jesus still touches the lives of receptive people, just as he did while walking the roads of Palestine, teaching beside the sea, and praying with the disciples on the mountain. Children are touched by Jesus when they hear the stories of his life among us, and they recognize their own feelings of love and helpfulness as the touch of Jesus rests upon their hearts. Our response as nurturing adults may be to open the doors for safe, enthusiastic self-giving on the part of children.

These are a few suggestions that will open these doors:

• Respect children's feelings by allowing them to offer worthwhile help. Many children are learning to crochet caps and scarves for the needy or for the victims of disasters. What fun to take yarn and directions to a nursing home where the child and elderly plan and make caps for others!

• Use everyday opportunities to help your child learn about Jesus and God's love. Note how often Jesus used the ritual of eating and sharing food as the setting for his teaching: at Peter's home with his friends, with the crowds at the seashore, with Mary and Martha and Lazarus, with the disciples who had been fishing, with the pilgrims on the road to Emmaus. Each time Jesus used the "teachable moment" to converse about what was at hand. His empathy for those who were sick, his understanding of those who were hungry, his own appreciation of friendship, his gifts of plenty rather than poverty—all of these speak to us and to our children of the awesome love and grace of God.

• Take time to give thanks. Most of the people whom Jesus touched were able to express their thanks. One leaped for joy; one hurried to make a good meal for Jesus. Children who see thankful adults learn to be grateful for every blessing. The common joys of home, food, and companionship are clearly among God's gracious gifts. To express thanks is to be touched yet again with Jesus' love.

Parents, grandparents, and others who nurture children will find their own lives touched by grace as our children, touched by Jesus, continue to grow in faith.

Questions for Discussion and Meditation

1. A recent study has shown that one out of every fifty children in the United States is homeless. This startling figure compels us to ask, *What can we do to help mend this major threat to those children and to our society, and what can we do right now for a homeless child?* Is there a homeless child in your children's class at school? Can you help provide clothing, school supplies, or food? How do you discuss this need with your children, or is it even fair to the homeless child to do so? How do you and your family share your conviction that all are children of God?

2. You may not be able to crochet, but what other projects could your family tackle that could help others who have touched their hearts? Is there a Habitat for Humanity project for which you could volunteer? take donations to the Lord's Cupboard or another local food bank? Can you volunteer as a helper or a storyteller at the public library or a school? Pay for a membership at the YMCA or YWCA for a family presently without a job?

3. Assure your children that prayer is a first response to hardship or emergency. What are the local issues for which your family might pray? What national or world issues deeply concern your family and church? Name issues of justice that demand correction.

WISDOM VERSUS KNOWLEDGE, AND WHY THE DIFFERENCE MATTERS
BIBLE READING: JAMES 3:13

"Grandma, show me a big word," said my favorite five-year-old. Carefully, I printed on her pad of paper *judicious*. Emily was just learning to read, and big words were mysterious and challenging.

"It means *wise*," I explained. "A judicious person thinks hard and uses good judgment about what she says and does." From then on, Emily and her little brother used the word generously. "Grandma, it would be *judicious* to have an ice ream bar because it is so hot today." "Grandma, I think it would be *judicious* to read lots more books before I go to sleep." It would be hard to reject a big word, but I did get a little tired of that one.

Years later, we discussed the difference between *knowledge* and *wisdom*. We considered some world leaders who had been brilliant, full of facts, and highly motivated to use them; but who did not make *judicious* decisions. How can a person develop both wisdom and knowledge? What is there in our culture that may hinder the development of wisdom?

The Bible has more than a little to say about it. We remember the Bible stories of King Solomon and his great wisdom. The Bible tells us clearly that all wisdom is from God. Only God's holy and divine mind can impart wisdom to humankind. What, then, is the wisdom of God when it comes to wise parenting and to the nurture of children?

The Book of James tell us that wisdom from above is utterly without a trace of partiality. Wise parents, grandparents, and teachers take that very much to heart. Comparing children negatively about their character, appearance, skills, or personality is fatal to peace in the family and probably in society as well. We have only to review the stories of dysfunctional families in the Bible to see the results of partiality or hypocrisy. Jacob, blessed by God in innumerable ways, no doubt suffered much from the disunity caused among his sons by his own partiality to the children of the beloved Rachel.

Some immigrants to our country came because the inheritance laws of their country were unfair or resulted in dispute among heirs to ancestral farmland. Resentment over favored treatment of one child may cause decades of troubled relationships among siblings.

Better we should be wise. We need to explain our actions and decisions to children and to examine our own hearts to be certain that we are fair and impartial.

Peace is also among those attributes of wisdom that the Bible advises. We are apt to tell our children not to hit, slap, or push; but at the same time we fail to offer ways to dissipate anger, even when anger seems justified. We have a Mad Tree here on the farm. A child who feels put out or even downright angry, is invited to go to the Mad Tree. There, the child can pound the ground, yell a little, shed a tear, or read a book under the shade of that friendly tree. The child judges for himself or herself when he or she is ready to leave the solace of the Mad Tree to seek the comfort of a listening adult or the companionship of siblings. Eventual maturity and wisdom result from such small steps. Children also gain in self-knowledge when they learn that they can overcome temper and exhibit self-control.

James tells us that wisdom from above is full of mercy and good fruits. Perhaps we think, *He's just a kid. What fruits could he produce?*

Encourage children to

- Help a grandmother or a neighbor with yard work.
- Put out a birdfeeder in the yard or garden.
- Grow a plant in a pot from seed to flower; take it to a teacher.
- Go through your books. Are there any that could cheerfully be given to a friend or to the library?
- Save some of their allowance until there is enough for a donation for "Nothing But Nets," the program that provides nets to protect African children from the mosquitoes that carry malaria.
- Help keep their Sunday school room clean. They can pick up papers, put away supplies, and stack books and Bibles neatly. They can learn not to expect the custodian to do everything.
- Practice good manners. They can say, "Good morning!" to an elderly person or listen carefully to the pastor and teachers.
- Encourage peaceful actions whenever possible, such as starting a Peace Club for Kids.

The list is inexhaustible. As children experience pleasure from being helpful and useful, they grow also in wisdom.

Knowledge is important. We need to know the multiplication tables before we can do sixth-grade math and, similarly, we need a reservoir of *knowledge* to undergird *wisdom*. As we encourage active, curious minds in our children, we must show every day how to use wisely the many facts gleaned in their studies.

Like Solomon, we pray daily that we as parents may gain wisdom. Surely, our greatest contribution is to encourage our children to follow in the steps of Jesus.

When it comes to being judicious, there is no better guide for any of us.

Questions for Discussion and Meditation

1. What factors do you feel may cause disparity between *knowledge* and *wisdom?*

2. When in your child-rearing experience have you wished or prayed for *wisdom?*

3. Look up *"wisdom"* in a concordance. Discuss some of the Bible verses. Choose a favorite wisdom verse to teach your children.

WHEN CHILDREN GRIEVE
BIBLE READING: ROMANS 8:28

This morning we awoke to an upper Midwestern storm of gargantuan proportions. A steady freezing rain had converted the landscape into a crystal wonderland. Five inches of light snow had sifted over the ice. Branches of the trees began to fall; the crack of their breaking woke me in the early morning to a scene of desolation. All around were broken trees and bushes bent to the ground under a burden of ice and snow.

Yet there was an awesome serenity in this scene. Each twig, each strand of fence, and each bowed branch glittered with dazzling beauty as the sun came out to end the storm. The sadness of destruction and the joy of beauty existed side by side in the morning panorama.

How often we walk hand in hand with both sadness and happiness in this life! Death of a dearly beloved one can be such a time, wintry in our soul. Yet spring is around the corner, and with it Easter—hope and new life.

An old friend of our church, who had left the community many years ago, returned one Sunday morning in a wheelchair. His daughter told us about his many illnesses. Her mother could no longer care for our friend, and the doctors had recommended a nursing home. Jill, a dedicated and compassionate nurse, chose instead to care for her parents in her own home.

I felt some misgivings, but quieted those by telling myself it was none of my business. Jill was a capable, skilled nurse with a good job and a lovely home. She and her husband still had young children at home, in addition to two older daughters. How was she to handle this, even with the help of her devoted husband?

With great difficulty seemed to be the answer. Our friend Al died a few weeks later. Joey and Chloe, five and seven years old, who had helped their parents and older sisters in the physical care of their grandfather, remained serene and cheerful. When my own life partner died shortly after their loss, the children came to me with hugs and smiles and assurances that God was in charge and loved me.

I wondered how the children had remained so serene and happy through those stressful weeks. "We did it together," said their mother. Sometimes, Chloe and Joey helped rub oil on Grandfather's back or feet. Sometimes they played games with him when he was able to sit in his wheelchair. Sometimes they helped wheel him around the ballpark or around the town square. Once they were able to take Grandpa to a family reunion, where he was able to see a beloved brother who was also in poor health. "They hugged each other," Joey reported.

"When I came home from school, he always asked, 'Is that my girl?'" declared Chloe. Sometimes she crawled up on his bed, which had been moved into the family room so that he could see the television with the family and share news of school.

"He liked to listen to the birds in the morning," added Joey. "Sometimes we went outside. Sometimes he just watched Grandma while she helped us with our 4-H projects. He was a good grandpa."

The children were not present when their grandfather died, but their parents awakened them an hour later as the family grieved and talked about Grandpa going away.

A few days later, the children found a cicada shell in the yard and carried it to their parents to see. This large fly-like insect develops as a nymph underground, emerging to the surface and shedding its outer skin as it becomes an adult cicada. The children marveled as they explained the whole thing to me, "Grandpa did not need his body anymore. He was like the cicada, which did not need the shell it had left behind. Grandpa left his body behind, but his real self was in heaven with Jesus. That's the way it is, Myrtle, and we will get to see him someday later on."

The children left our interview with hugs and smiles. They said they cried when Grandpa died and Grandma went back to her home, but they knew Grandpa still loved them. They remembered the cicada that left behind what it did not need.

Like our wintry morning, sadness and beauty accompany the death of a loved one. Children feel grief that is deep and real, just like the rest of us; but wise parents can guide the grieving process, helping children feel the beauty and hope of life everlasting with Jesus.

Questions for Discussion and Meditation

1. Children who have seen sudden, unexpected death may not handle it as well as Chloe and Joey, who had weeks of preparation for this parting; and cicada shells may not be so easily found! What metaphors might you use in comforting and reassuring young children after the death of a loved one?

2. Children's grief may find expression in unacceptable behavior, in withdrawal, or simply in confusion and uncertainty. When the parents are also in deep grief, the special needs of the surviving children may be overlooked. How can the church help with grieving families? Is this a job just for the pastor? How have you dealt with your own grief in similar circumstances?

3. At what age should children be expected to attend funeral services? funeral home visitation? home visits? Is there another way for children to express sympathy and grief? How can the adults in the home or church help with a child's grief process? How does our Bible verse for today help us and our children deal with grief?

PART THREE
SPRING AND SUMMER
GREENING TREES

CAN TRUST BE TAUGHT?
BIBLE READING: PROVERBS 3:5-6

"Gwandma," said a small voice on the phone, "I just thought you would want to know that I feel puny today."

I certainly did want to know if my three-year-old grandson was feeling ill. Kyle knew that he could ask Grandma to say a prayer, come over with his favorite soup and cookies, and stay to read some books. Kyle trusted his Grandma to do whatever she could to make him comfortable on a day when he felt puny.

Parents and grandparents can become loving, trustworthy persons, knowing that "We love because he first loved us" (1 John 4:19). We can trust God to know our hearts and to do always what is best for us. Teaching about such trust to our children is a long-time effort. It requires that primary caregivers (parents, grandparents, teachers) prove themselves always to be trustworthy. How else could a child define or identify real trust? Sometimes we say, "Trust me" merely to signify what we think is true or what we want a listener to accept as true. But every day, whether we say it or not, we are indicating "Trust me" to our children. Are we carrying through?

There are many stories that show us how our Bible friends trusted God. Noah did not hesitate to build a huge boat in the backyard, even though it seemed silly at the time. Abraham did not hesitate to go where God instructed him to go; he just packed up his herds and his family and set out into the unknown. Mary said, "let it be with me according to your word" (Luke 1:38) when told that she would be the mother of the Savior.

One of our favorite stories tells of Moses and the Israelites crossing the Sea of Reeds on their flight from Egypt. Can you imagine the courage it took to step into that seabed? What if the wind stopped blowing the waters back, and God let the waves cover the whole people of Israel!

We, too, often have to step into the unknown, trusting our God to carry out God's divine purpose for us. Not long ago I stood on the steep bank of the Chariton River, where early pioneers crossed during a flood. It was necessary for them to pull some of the wagons and animals up the riverbank with ropes. Yet every single settler arrived safely and camped on the verdant meadow beyond the river. Today, I cross that river on a sturdy bridge; and in time of flood the waters swirl safely beneath me. Yet in the midst of the flood, I forget neither the faith of the Israelites nor the faith of our forebears who journeyed to this green land. We can trust God.

Children who step confidently into the future, sure of God's care, strong in their trust and faith, have probably seen such trust and confidence in their family life. It is not that the family has never encountered crises, it is how we allow God to lead us through crises that counts. A lost job, a serious illness, a fractured friendship, a neighborhood quarrel—we can be sure that our children note how these and other situations are handled by the adults, and that it affects their own growth in faith and trust.

Our children must be able to trust that we will do what we say we will do, whether that is an ice cream party on a birthday or being grounded for breaking rules. A young mother makes promises to her children, none of which she keeps, so their behavior never improves. Toning down and following through might convince her children to trust her in other situations as well.

Accountability is a sign of maturity. That applies to parents and other adults in a child's life as well as to the growing child. We need to be accountable for our budget if we expect children to be accountable with their lunch money. We must be accountable for our chores if we expect children to be accountable with their homework. Even preschoolers can put their tricycles away or see that their toys are not on sidewalks or in hallways at the end of the day. Habit and gentle reminders help us all to be accountable and responsible, which in turn lead to greater trust relationships.

Unfortunately, we also need to look at distrust issues. Our children must be cautioned against getting into cars without parental permission, against talking with persons unknown to them, against uncomfortable touching. "Stranger danger" is very real and cannot be ignored. Clear guidelines, lovingly enforced, clarify the issue for children and give them confidence.

> *The best ingredient in the trust recipe is the unconditional love that primary caretakers give to children, just as God's unconditional love sustains and strengthens us.*

The best ingredient in the trust recipe is the unconditional love that primary caretakers give to children, just as God's unconditional love sustains and strengthens us. We can never be too busy or distracted to give attention to our children's needs. A little boy was coloring a picture in my vacation Bible school class. When I reminded the children that it was time for recreation, he said, "Hold on; I'll be with you in a minute." It is perfectly okay for either the child or the parent to ask someone to "hold on," providing it is not an emergency. I am confident that this boy trusted his teacher not to be annoyed, and I know the teacher trusted Chad to hurry up! Both of us knew we would soon turn our attention to this matter.

Patience, understanding, empathy, justice, love—these and many other factors go into trust relationships among humans. How much more, then, do we trust our Creator, who offers divine understanding, who cares deeply and individually for each of us! Children who see our trust in God, who experience trust in family and community relationships, will respond to the prevenient love of God with confidence and faith. Trust me.

Questions for Discussion and Meditation

1. Have you ever been distrusted, especially by someone you love? How did you earn back their confidence?

Photo by Stephen Gardner

2. Do your church members ever exhibit distrust for the leaders of the congregation or the judiciary bodies of the denomination? If so, how do you proceed?

3. Who are the most trusted people in your life? in your children's lives?

LEARNING THROUGH NATURE
BIBLE READING: PSALM 24:1-2

The red-tailed hawk swooped over the barn and perched in a tall snag of a cottonwood tree.

"He's back! Grandpa's hawk is back!" shouted the children.

We never named that hawk, though we knew him well. Each year when the soil first began to smell spring-sweet and Grandpa was itching to get the machinery to the field, that red-tailed hawk arrived to help with the farming. He followed the machinery in the fields, swooping down to capture whatever mouse, vole, or rabbit was scared up. Many of those he carried off to the timber, where we assumed he had a mate and a nest. That was one ambitious hawk. All summer he moved from field to field, capturing dinner.

Later in the fall, when the nippy air promised winter, the hawk would disappear, probably to the river where the water remained open during cold weather. But as he left, Grandpa's hawk made one last swoop over the field, flying directly in front of the combine cab as he did each evening, as though to say to Grandpa, "That's all for now. You're on your own."

We learned a lot from Grandpa's hawk, beside the obvious lesson of taking advantage of God-given opportunities. The strength, beauty, and persistence of the hawk challenged us in our own daily work. His ability to form even such a tenuous relationship with another creature gave us pause; how willing were we to form relationships under such conditions of uncertainty and risk? The children and I pondered a lot over that hawk, who paid us no attention whatsoever as he carried his prey to the nestlings day after day. Grandpa Paul marked the seasons with his friend the hawk.

Learning from nature is not new, by any means. In recent decades, Howard Gardner, professor and author from Harvard University, has named Naturalist as one of the basic ways in which we gather and process information. This basic intelligence enabled our earliest ancestors to succeed as farmers, hunters, and gatherers. Many of our Bible friends used this ability in order to form cooperative groups and to establish families and clans. We remember the nomads and the herders of early Bible times, among them Abraham, Isaac, and Jacob. King David certainly used his linguistic, mathematical, and musical abilities as king; but those were nurtured as a shepherd boy who guarded, nourished, and led his sheep beside still waters and greening meadows. Nature has always provided the means of life, but it is obvious that it also nurtures ways of thinking and responding to life and its many mysteries.

In this post-modern age, however, many of our children are removed from opportunities to interact or even observe the workings of nature. Since recognizing and naming the creative work of God is one of the early tasks of faith formation, parents, grandparents, and teachers have the awesome task of introducing children to nature in as many ways as possible.

Jesus often used the beauty of God's creation in his teaching. "Consider the lilies of the field," he said, "even Solomon in all his glory was not clothed like one of these. But if God so clothes the grass of the field, which is alive today and tomorrow is thrown into the oven, will he not much more clothe you—you of little faith?" (Matthew 6:28-30). Jesus pointed out that we can rely on God's ultimate and eternal care for us. Understanding the land is central to understanding the culture of Bible times. Jesus refers to the sower who plants his seed and the enemy who sows weeds in the field, and he refers often to the harvest. All of these metaphors are perhaps less understandable to many children today, so we must find ways to interpret those customs and apply those truths to their lives.

> ## *Jesus often used the beauty of God's creation in his teaching.*

I once measured off a square foot of lawn for each of my grandchildren to inspect, with the goal of finding the many things God had placed in that square foot of land. We found bugs, earthworms, grass, tiny weeds—and, yes, here was a tiny fragment of a gum wrapper! We knew that once that paper wrapper had been a part of a tree, and we were awed at the thought that God's creation would come full cycle, returning that paper to soil that would nourish a new tree. How wondrous are God's ways! Here was a miracle indeed!

There are innumerable indoor activities that can nurture a child's love for nature. I keep a file of beautiful colored pictures cut from magazines or printed from the computer. Visiting children enjoy sorting and classifying them into various categories: animals from different continents; animals of earth, sky, or sea; meat-eating animals versus those that eat grass and vegetation; animals that enjoy insects; domestic animals and wild animals. Sometimes we cut some of the pictures into puzzles, mix up all the pieces, and time ourselves as we assemble them again. Sometimes we need to get on the computer to answer questions about the animals, another wonderful mix of learning styles. In every case, we wonder at the creative majesty of our God.

We can work wonders with a little potting soil and some grass seed. My Sunday school class loves to cut the tops off plastic milk jugs, leaving five or six inches of the bottom to hold potting soil. We use felt markers to make a face on the plastic, sow grass in the soil, water it, and put it on a window sill. Gradually, our plastic person grows some green hair. What has God wrought!

Or we fill a small glass jar with soil, tucking a bean seed close to the glass so it can be watched. We water, wait, and soon the children see the miracle of sprout and growth through the glass. The best learning takes place as we talk with our children about related Bible stories and about the awesome nature of our creative God.

We are seeing a new adaptation of the "dude ranch" as a place for families from the city to vacation. Working farms are sometimes open to vacations where families can actually help with the haying, animal care, riding farm machinery, and eating scrumptious meals from the farm kitchen. There are many parks and walking trails that encourage us to enjoy nature and the presence of God in the beautiful outdoors. Our learning is enhanced by this time together.

When we are hiking or playing, we just might see a hawk swooping over the land or perched on a tall tree. Say, "hi," just in case it's Grandpa's hawk.

Questions for Discussion and Meditation

1. How have you and your children related to nature today? this week?

2. Have you ever attended a county or state fair? a cattle auction? a birdwatching hike? What might you and your children expect to learn?

3. How responsible has your family been in the use of energy, natural resources, preservation of birds or animals? What might you do? What does God expect?

Thinking Independently
Bible Reading: Matthew 22:37-38

"Grandma, why can I have a penny for my thoughts? I'm thinking all the time!" declared my solemn four-year-old grandchild as we trudged up a timber hill.

True, this kid talked a lot; and most of it seemed reasonable. He loved the books we read (incessantly, it seemed to Grandma), the stories we told, and the matters of grave concern that we discussed. (Why are girls afraid of dogs and snakes? Why aren't there dinosaurs in the timber? Why can't we see God, if God is everywhere?)

Independent thinking and impossible questions can be worrisome to some parents. We want our children to think as we think, accept the values that we accept, act according to family standards rather than on impulse. One of my own mother's favorite expressions was "Use your head!" Having been trained to think independently, I wondered about the value of passing this along.

The teachings of parents and Sunday school teachers are always respected and cherished, but we must expect that sometimes the young will hear the message in different ways.

Many of us live an unexamined faith. We accept and believe what our parents, our Sunday school teachers, and even our culture have presented to us. Some, however, both live and examine their faith-response in ways that lead to owned faith, a faith that is rock-firm, on which we can base our entire lives. Helping children and youth move toward that owned faith means we must not only permit, we must encourage, independent thinking, fearsome as it sounds. The teachings of parents and Sunday school teachers are always respected and cherished, but we must expect that sometimes the young will hear the message in different ways.

It is easy to teach the facts. We know the family tree of Cain, Abel, Abraham, Sarah, Ishmael, Isaac, Rebekah, Jacob, and Esau. Our Sunday school lessons examine their faith, their travels, the presence of God in their lives, even when they made awesome mistakes. Even the youngest of our children know that this family from the Bible was a troubled family. What lies behind the discord? Why does conflict rule so many generations of this family? Why did God choose this family? Children may need help to identify jealousy, favoritism, and sibling rivalry as the very human causes of their problems and for most of the problems that families experience today. How does learning to think independently help?

A sixth-grade Sunday school teacher summoned me to her classroom one Sunday morning. It seemed that the students had read in the Sunday paper of a man in California who walked too close to the shore and was seized by a shark that had penetrated the shark guard. When the shark was finally captured, all that remained in the stomach was a belt buckle and the soles of the man's shoes. "Explain," urged the kids, "how Jonah could have lived three days in the belly of a big fish, if this one digested a human being in 24 hours."

Hey, I was confident about this one!

"In the first place, God, who made the Big Fish, could stop the digestive juices of the Big Fish, if God wanted to." I let that soak in a moment before I added, "But I'm not certain that's what happened. The purpose of the whole incident was to show us that God wanted Jonah in Nineveh, and there is no running away from God. So how else might he have gotten there?"

These kids were wonderful. "Maybe it wasn't so far, and he swam." "Maybe a friendly dolphin passed by and gave him a ride." "Maybe another fishing boat came along and took him there." "Maybe one of the guys on the boat hauled him in secretly."

Once encouraged, they were willing to think independently of all the possibilities, including that God stopped the digestive juices of the Big Fish. In the end, we agreed that the Bible story was not about Jonah and the "whale" at all, but about answering God's call and doing God's will. We prayed for the family of the California man with the belt buckle and thanked God for many blessings.

Independent thinking is an acquired skill that enhances the growing maturity of our children. There are those who run with the crowd or are swayed by passionate rhetoric or perhaps even by playground bullying. Even unfortunate incidents must be carefully examined by parent and child together, without prejudgment or anger.

To encourage independent thinking, ask these questions:
- What factors led to your decision to take part in the incident? Expect answers such as, "The other kids were doing it," "I just wanted to have fun," or "I didn't think it was wrong."
- What were the consequences of this mistake? Was anyone harmed?
- What might you have done differently?
- What might have been the consequences of this different action?
- How will you decide the next time someone suggests a doubtful activity?
- What role does prayer have when we are confused or uncertain or tempted?

Honest and loving communication between parent and child enables a child to own up to mistakes; think creatively in a pinch; and trust his or her decisions will find support, or at least understanding. We grownups expect the same from our spouses and friends. Why should kids expect anything less?

God gives us a brain. Jesus tells us, "You shall love the Lord your God with all your heart, and with all your soul, and with all your mind" (Matthew 22:37). That must mean that we use those brains to help us follow Jesus, to make godly choices, and to do good in the world. I am sure God nodded approval when my own mother said, "Use your head!"

Questions for Discussion and Meditation

1. Name a belief or a fact that you were taught in your childhood, one about which you are now ambivalent. How did you come to question this belief? Is it a matter of interpretation? experience? How can you determine who is "right"? Should you try to make such a determination?

2. How do you handle it when your child or youth questions your values or beliefs? Is this evidence of independent thinking threatening to you? Why?

3. Compare Deuteronomy 6:5 with Matthew 22:37-38. How do you account for this difference? What is the meaning in each case?

On Valuing the Marginal
Bible Reading: James 2:8-9

There was a difference of opinion in our family about Ol' Lop-Ears. My husband originally felt that we should sell her; her ears were put on backwards and possibly this characteristic would be carried forward in her calves. It did not seem like good business to have a lop-eared cow in the herd. Nevertheless, she was my favorite cow, gentle and curious, and the Chief Herdsman agreed to pamper me. We kept Ol' Lop-Ears, and each year she raised a perfect calf. Nature is unpredictable, and perhaps we need to learn that we need not try to fix everything.

This year, after a wonderful spring of enjoying numerous colorful birds at our feeders and birdbaths, we suffered an unexpected invasion—bees. We definitely wanted to protect the bees, whose numbers are diminishing throughout the country. However, it was not long before the bees had chased away the orioles and even the grosbeaks.

This niche in our bird population was quickly filled—you guessed it—by the house sparrows. I resigned myself to watching their interaction with the bees, even as they quickly liquidated my supply of birdseed. It soon became evident that this undervalued little bird was rather clever. He cracked a sunflower seed as quickly as the grosbeak, then perched on the clothesline until a young sparrow made a wobbly landing beside him. The nestling opened his beak; and the adult popped the kernel into his mouth, right there on the clothesline. The humble house sparrow, the least valued of birds, cohabitated with the bees and raised his nestlings without problems. Both the sparrow and Ol' Lop-Ears had a place in the life and ecology of our farm.

I began to think of the "marginal" children in our community, the ones overlooked because they are not as popular, talented, colorful, or privileged as others. As one of the poorer counties in our state, we are third highest in the number of abused children. The closing of manufacturing plants has brought crises to many families. I asked one wage-earner how secure his job might be. "We could shut down any time," he said. "Most families don't buy anything we don't absolutely need." His children are decently clothed and well-fed. His neighbor, however, is unemployed. They visit the Lord's Cupboard for essential groceries, rely on a county educational group for school supplies and lunches. Their home is in jeopardy, their children becoming invisible as attention is focused on the brightest, the talented, the more fortunate children of the community. Unfortunately, communities with these problems exist all over America and the world.

Are we missing something here? Is any child marginal, or are they, like Ol' Lop Ears and the newly appreciated sparrows, under recognized, under utilized, under noticed, and under motivated? What hope and accomplishments for the future are we missing if we fail to identify and encourage the marginal children of our communities? As parents and Christians, we share responsibility for the welfare of all children. None are invisible in the eyes of God.

As I drove through a nearby town one day, I waved at a group of children on a street corner. One responded by shouting insulting words. (About my age and beauty—can you imagine!) These may be the very children you have not wanted your own child to play with. What is a Christian to do?

The problem is best tackled by groups sponsored by a church, community center, or by an organized group of parents. Be sure that all children are included in these activities. By learning to know and value everyone, all lives will be enriched.

One church located on spacious grounds has organized softball teams for all the children of the neighborhood. Sponsors actively recruit the less privileged children; a junior high coach gives many summer hours to instruct and oversee this program.

- A pilot who has built his own plane visits youth camps every summer to share the building process with the kids. He also gives airplane rides every spring to the graduates of the tween Sunday school class in his church. Why not offer a Model Airplane Club, where children of the neighborhood may receive some help and encouragement with model planes? The local airport manager or the Experimental Aircraft Association chapter might want to help with this plan!

- Plan for tutoring. This could be done after school in the church building or a community center. Contact a local school for help in organizing and recruiting. Expect all tutors to have background checks. Discover the special interests and abilities of all the children, plan a fun event every month or every quarter. Enable all the children to know their way around the building and to feel welcome and comfortable there.

- If you can find a spot of ground for a garden, recruit children to help with a neighborhood project. Engage them in preparing the soil, choosing seeds, pulling weeds, watering or fertilizing, harvesting the vegetables or flowers, delivering the harvest to those who need them, taking some home for the use of their own families, or even selling them, thus enabling the children to contribute to other missions. At every stage, you can find a Bible verse or story that fits these efforts. You will be laboring together, but you can also be theologizing (thinking about God.) In a day when this does not happen in the majority of homes, talking about God as you work will matter.

- Organize a backyard Fine Arts Festival. Some of these community events draw only the children already identified as gifted. Make yours a ground zero event where the motive is to discover every child's interest and provide opportunities to develop a gift. In one church, a talented musician taught a child elementary skills on the piano, a pastor took a boy fishing, another helped the kids make puppets and write puppet plays about their worries and concerns. In each case, the establishment of trust relationships was paramount; and children were helped to walk as disciples of Jesus as well as to discover their own special gifts.

- Have you tried an after-school pizza party? I cannot think of anything that draws more enthusiastic kids than pizza. Only difference is, this time you provide the ingredients and allow the children to assemble and bake their own pizzas, including extras to take as gifts to the elderly or to any family in the neighborhood who might enjoy a pizza for supper. (I identify these neighbors or friends ahead of time, alerting them to expect supper.) Giving is itself a spiritual gift, one  that many children have not experienced. Do it joyfully, have fun, and be sure to clean up the church kitchen before you leave.

There are children who are hungry for the attention of caring Christian adults. Though we see children from many walks of life, acknowledge that there are no marginal children in God's eyes. We walk together on the disciple path, praying for the transformation of the whole world with every small step.

Questions for Discussion and Meditation

1. What efforts does your church make to be hospitable and inclusive? What efforts do you make as an individual?

2. How can attitudes of entitlement be changed? for privileged children? for the unfortunate?

3. What evidence can you give that God's love is impartial?

4. Define *love* in one sentence.

CHILDREN AND SELF-CONTROL
BIBLE READING: 2 PETER 1:6-7

I watched as my grandson contrived a rubber band gun to shoot at a target fence post at our farm home. The project consisted of a clothespin, a stick of wood, a paper clip, and yards and yards of masking tape. Eventually, a handful of rubber bands peppered the ground around the fence post.

"It works," he said with satisfaction as he pointed out the directions in his favorite magazine.

His sense of satisfaction certainly reinforced his image of himself as a capable person. Even more importantly, such emotional satisfaction is one of the factors that leads to self-control in children.

Dr. Roy Baumeister from Florida State University suggests in a recent study that self-control is restored through positive emotional experiences as well as through adequate sleep and self-regulatory exercises. The exact mechanism of self-control is unknown, but it is evident that it is flexible. There are times when a child may exercise great self-control and other times when things go amuck. So how can we consistently encourage growth in will power and self-discipline in our children?

Most families live in very busy households. Busyness need not be chaos, however. Schedules and boundaries give a child a sense of security. If the occasional chaos is met with little fuss, the child registers that the unusual or unexpected can be handled with poise.

Listen carefully to children. One young boy told me his grandma was nice. "She doesn't really play with me, but she comes and looks at stuff when I ask her to." How little it takes to assure a child that she or he is valued! The valued child, the self-confident child, is also the child who has greater control of his or her emotions and actions.

An increase nationally in overweight children may direct our attention to how a child may learn self-control in personal habits. Every child, for instance, needs adequate sleep. A walk or a quiet game before bedtime and a warm shower and soft music may encourage restful sleep. Many parents recognize that the child who is rested and properly nourished has the edge on self-control.

For some people, it is helpful to monitor one's food intake in writing. Perhaps, with the help of parents, children can adapt this food control method. A parent may suggest a chart, urging the child to record junk food or other no-nos in red and nutritional, balanced foods in green. Keeping the chart can be the child's responsibility. When weight loss is recorded, the emotional satisfaction is not only a triumph for health, it is a factor in future behaviors that require self-control, including overeating. Self-image is enhanced when the chart shows more green than red, even though weight loss is not immediately apparent.

Self-control also results from experiences of trust in matters appropriate to the age of the child. Personally, this grandmother and teacher believes in rites of passage and big kids parties. The neighborhood children are welcome to play in our yard. There are swing sets, ball diamonds, and trees to climb, all of which a child may use without supervision once she or he is old enough to come to a big kids party. Other places, deemed high adventure, require my permission and supervision. Of course, as with any other setting, some places are absolutely forbidden.

No one gets in a tizzy because these rules cannot be bent. These are the big kids who respond to my expectation that they are reliable and trustworthy. If a child loses his or her cool over a game or in an argument over rules, the child is entitled to relax under the maple tree until the child feels like himself or herself again. We end these playtimes before exhaustion sets in, thereby preserving everyone's good nature and setting the stage for another day.

All children need to have their own interests and goals accepted as important by the family, and all children need the experience of offering support to parents and siblings. Problems centering around homework, care of pets, procrastination, truth-telling, or just the competition that may arise in family life need everyone's cooperation and contribution in finding variable solutions.

As children grow in self-control in even one area of life, they are less likely to be susceptible to addictive behavior as youths or adults. The watchful and sincere encouragement of parents and teachers while children are young bears great fruit in later years.

Questions for Discussion and Meditation

1. What are the unusual or unexpected circumstances that your child has had to handle lately? Was the situation handled well? Did self-control enter into the equation?

2. Addictive behavior is all around us. What does your family do to minimize the attraction of drugs, alcohol, or other addictive behaviors or substances? What did Paul mean by "sober judgment" (Romans 12:3)?

FROM MY WEST WINDOW
BIBLE READING: MATTHEW 28:18-20

It is early morning; and I am lost in thought as I gaze at the yard, the fields, the timbered hills beyond, just greening up for spring. Out in the cornstalks a newly arrived flock of male red-winged black-birds pick at last fall's spilled grain. The swing set in the yard hangs limp. I remember the day we braced that swing in cement to accommodate the growing grandchildren. Now the youngest reaches up, grasps the top, and uses it as an exercise bar. Growth and change and promise are all around us, even as the juncos gather for their next flight.

As we trace the earthly ministry of Jesus, there are reminders along the way that can help us in our own nurturing journey with children.

The spring Sunday school lessons twang at the cords of my being. "Remembering Jesus." How can we possibly forget him in the midst of this unfolding seasonal promise? Perhaps, as parents and grandparents, we face the reality of our own forgetfulness, the teachable moments that we often miss in the busyness of our days. As we trace the earthly ministry of Jesus, there are reminders along the way that can help us in our own nurturing journey with children.

A third-grader in our community saw with horror the pictures of the tsunami of December, 2004. The sight of the crushed buildings, the huge waves carrying away property and lives, and the despair of the families who survived touched the heart of this little girl. She began to make wooden earrings and pins that she gave to her teachers and friends for a contribution for tsunami victims. She alone was able to send more than a hundred dollars for tsunami aid. Her actions helped us remember that "[Jesus] . . . went about doing good" (Acts 10:38); and we, too, began to give freely toward this special need.

Though it was not difficult for Jesus, we humans sometimes wonder what we can do to help those who are ill. We send cards and say prayers; but only recently was it made clear to me how precious is the loving, personal gesture in times of great uncertainty. When my husband had unexpected open-heart surgery, I had to be gone from my elementary Sunday school class for several weeks. During that time, the children in my class sent us a chain of construction paper rings that I hung over my computer. Daily I was reminded that we are all linked together, that these boys and girls cared about my husband; and that they realized that I needed their love and support, too. Many greetings arrived, but none more precious than that chain of construction paper rings that will probably hang above my computer forever!

We need to be connected with children; we remember that Jesus loved and valued children. We remember Jesus best when we try to act as Jesus would. We cannot heal the sick in the ways Jesus did, but gestures of love can help others.

Friendships, too, should not be taken for granted. Tiffs among children may be expected; even the disciples, grown men, had a few disagreements. Nevertheless, the bonds of friendship should never be taken lightly. There was an old song that went, "Make new friends, but keep the old. One is silver, and the other's gold." Childhood friendships that stand the test of time, even in our very mobile society, can be precious indeed. Jesus valued his friends; he went to a wedding feast, often had picnics along the lakeshore, and visited the homes of his friends and ate meals with them. Imagine what fun they must have had! Jesus and his disciples enjoyed many good times together, and I am sure that Jesus told many other good stories that we do not even know. One Gospel writer tells us that if all the stories about Jesus were written down, probably the whole world could not hold the books! So we can easily assume that Jesus and his friends walked up the hills to the Temple in Jerusalem, singing songs of praise and thanksgiving to God. What a great time Jesus had with his friends!

Sharing these insights with our children helps them to cherish friendships, just as Jesus did, and to cultivate those early friendships as they mature.

Remembering Jesus is not complete until we recall his spiritual and devotional life. Jesus often prayed. He asked God to heal the sick, he drew aside to the mountaintop to commune with God, and he attended the synagogue on the sabbath "as was his habit" to read the Hebrew Scriptures and to discuss them with other adults. Because Jesus communed so often with his Father God, we too see the vitality of prayer. We need to pray with children, to retell the Bible stories, and to visualize the risen Jesus with us at every moment of our days.

Perhaps the most important thing we do as we remember Jesus is to love and serve him as our resurrected Lord. We remember what Jesus taught us through his words and deeds and that he overcame sin and death. This is not difficult to share with children in the springtime when we see the evidence all around us. A tulip grows in the yard, from bulb to bloom in such a short time. Two geese fly over at treetop level, honking out their discovery of a clear pond with nesting reeds along the banks. Children jump rope with giddy persistence; and families walk in the city park, pushing strollers with babies. What new life Jesus brings to us all, through his glorious presence and in the renewal of the earth!

Remembering Jesus is like remembering to breathe. He is part and parcel of our very life.

Questions for Discussion and Meditation

1. Children may be familiar with the four seasons of the calendar year. Do you know that there is a Christian year fashioned on the life of Jesus? What season of the Christian year are we in at this time? How will you explain this Christian season to the children? Is it important to do so?

2. Spring traditionally means new beginnings. What new beginning is needed in the life of your family? your congregation? your personal life?

THE HOT SAUCE QUEEN AND OTHER HEROES AND HEROINES
BIBLE READING: GALATIANS 5:13-14

It is hard to anticipate who will be the heroes and heroines of today's children. Many diverse factors influence their daily thinking, feeling, and deciding. Individuals who have gained fame, power, publicity, or wealth seem to be popular role models. Most children would like to possess at least one of those.

A *hero* could be defined as "anyone admired for his or her qualities or achievements and regarded as an ideal or model." But who does that include?

My vote is with the Hot Sauce Queen. Now eighty years old, retired from a successful career as a writer and editor of children's curriculum materials, Jean Buchanan goes each week to Edgehill United Methodist Church in Nashville, Tennessee, to help serve meals to people who are homeless. She is affectionally known by many as the Hot Sauce Queen, as she faithfully greets and serves hot sauce to many people. Age and health do not stop Jean from being our heroine, though she would never define herself that way. Jean has spent her life in service to others.

On the last play of a close football bowl game (score 25-34, with Iowa down), an Iowa Hawkeye senior caught a 56-yard pass and raced for a touchdown—his first one in his college football career. A hero? I'll say! Thousands of Iowa kids dream of growing up to be someone like this young man on the football field.

The question is, Do parents have any influence on their children's choice of heroes or heroines? Obsession with celebrities can lead to problems for our children and youth. Helping them choose role models wisely is one of the challenges of parenthood.

- Help your children develop relationships with people who are living faithful Christian lives, helping others, and taking part in church and civic responsibilities. Help them know the fire-fighter and police officer who keep them safe, the farmer who grows the food they eat, the county or parish supervisors who make important decisions that immediately affect the lives of citizens. Help them know the conservation officer, the street cleaner, the forester, and the recycling worker who help sustain a good environment. Perhaps they will realize that the important heroes are not movie actors or multimillion-dollar entertainers, but the people at the crossroads of daily life who serve a larger purpose.

- Share biographies and history about worthy heroes. Read to your children, often choosing stories or articles around real people and their adventures. There are exciting children's books about Marco Polo, George Washington, Kate Shelley, Peter Cartwright, Harriet Tubman, Elizabeth Browning, and many others.

- Discuss parts of the daily news with your children. Hopefully, this can happen at the dinner table or some other place where the whole family has an opportunity to be together. Ask questions and offer opinions. *How do you feel about the actions of this person? What would be a better way to solve this problem? How could the church help in the situation we read about in today's paper?* Identify the people you admire.

- Monitor your child's television viewing. There are television shows during primetime evening hours that are rife with immoral sexual innuendo, incessant family quarreling, aggressive behavior, and violence. Young children are quick to model what they see.

- Look for heroes and heroines in new places. Try the History Channel. Click onto public television. Rent a movie. Take up bird watching. Learn to skate. Rent a horse. Walk around a lake. Volunteer. Sing with a choir. Take your family to a good concert. See a play together. Play an instrument. Try ballet. Television does not have to dominate a family's free time, and heroes and heroines may be found in many other places.

Children love to be around people of courage and tenacity with a sense of humor and a zest for living—people like the Hot Sauce Queen. Jean long ago patterned her life after Jesus, who "went about doing good." Just ask some of the children who were in Jean's Sunday school class. They loved her laugh. They loved her commitment, and many of them have since followed her example.

Questions for Discussion and Meditation

1. Who are the real-life heroes or heroines you remember? What actions or values attracted your attention? Did you adopt some of this person's characteristics? How has this hero or heroine been an influence in your life? Name concrete examples.

2. Who are the Bible heroines and heroes you admire? David as a courageous war leader? (He also sinned greatly.) Paul, the traveling apostle? (He seemed prejudiced against women.) Lydia, the businesswoman? (Was she the author of one of the Epistles?) Why was Jonah included in the canon?

3. What difference have you made in the lives of others? Do you agree with Nelson Mandela's statement? Why or why not? How would you share this understanding with your children?

WASTE NOT, WANT NOT
BIBLE READING: PROVERBS 21:5

Benjamin Franklin—diplomat, inventor, kite-flyer—was never more effective than when he compiled his accumulated wisdom in *Poor Richard's Almanac.* Certainly, today, many environmental problems, as well as personal problems, might have been alleviated by less waste and less want. This is probably true in many other areas of our lives.

Some of us remember the childhood admonition, "Clean your plate. Some little child in China might be going hungry." I never figured out how rejecting spinach would harm some Chinese child, but I did realize that waste includes more than food. Time, intellect, personal energy, all of these are gifts of God and meant to be used wisely.

Time for a child is not the same as for an adult. Of course, there are occasions when tasks are accomplished and time is scheduled. The child on overload, however, is just as vulnerable to value-deprivation as the child with no responsibilities at all. Childhood is a time for learning, playing, exploring, and being. It is a time for expecting, planning, reacting, rejecting, attempting, and rejoicing. A clergyman once declared that he felt sorry for the child who never had to help hay get in before it rained. Dreaming and working often go hand in hand, and we do not want to deprive our children of the privileges of both.

But what about taking the time to dream? That is hardly within our modern understanding. Such time is not wasted, however, so long as it does not divert the child from reality. Wasted time for a child is more likely to be the overload that either parents or peers expect. There are gifted children who want to play every horn in the band; but usually it is more productive for the child to spend time on one instrument, plus a little dream-time. Wasted time might also be excessive television watching or excessive time playing electronic games. Those activities may be positive, but they may also be destructive if time is not limited by the parent. Never confuse wasted time with needed recreation!

A waste of personal energy may seem trivial. Energy wasted in anger, revenge, trickery, or jealousy certainly drains us of motivation, but also damages our character. Actually, it can be very difficult to redirect these emotions; children sometimes need help with techniques of control. As a child, my fits of annoyance at my peers were met with my mother's calm words, "Forgive it. Maybe his mother never taught him any different." We both overlooked the fact that this might unfairly blame a parent, but it did serve to remind me that growing up is a learning process. We are obliged to teach our children better ways to deal with frustration, and this means sharing their pain. *A parent's work is never done!*

Physical energy is personal. Some of us have a much greater supply than others. Encourage physical movement as much as possible. Exercise should be an important part of growing up. A ten-year-old couch potato is wasting both health and opportunity. There is much concern in the news lately about the national epidemic of overweight or obese childhood. God surely means for children to enjoy lively, health-sustaining activities that in turn provide us with more energy throughout our lives.

Probably, Benjamin Franklin was thinking mostly of money and goods when he wrote those words of wisdom; and certainly that reflects some important biblical understandings.

Sharing is the opposite of waste. A wonderful story is told in an old newspaper from southern Iowa. A century ago, there were many coal mines in the area, each mine having a miner's town made up of small square houses in which the miners and their families lived. The company store, similar to the one in the song "Sixteen Tons," was available for buying the most essential groceries. The miners never worked in the summer when there was no demand for coal, so they spent this time gardening and hunting, laying up canned supplies for winter. One summer, a severe drought dried up the gardens and pastures; farmers were chopping down trees to allow their cattle to eat the leaves. Children in the miner's town became thin and lethargic. One caring farmer went to the company store with an offer: If the company would supply flour for the miner's wives to make bread, the farmer would butcher beef for the villagers. The children of the mining town received food until the miners returned to work. This story of caring and God's providence is still told over a century later. How much better than storing up riches in barns and banks!

We are often told stories of the early Native American use of the buffalo. No part was wasted! Even the tail was used as either a fly swatter or boiled for soup. Other stories, however, speak of the waste of the buffalo by both Native Americans and the white settlers and cowboys. Sometimes whole herds of buffalo were driven off a cliff, then only the choice parts harvested while most of the animal was wasted. White hunters later ruthlessly killed whole herds. As a result of this indiscriminate waste, the buffalo all but disappeared; and the Native American population fell as this source of food was eliminated. What a waste! I believe that Benjamin Franklin would have lifted his eyebrows in disapproval at that one, and I also think God grieved at this waste of bounty.

These are the types of true stories that both instruct and inspire our children. There are wonderful accounts of missionaries driving a herd of reindeer across Alaska to relieve the hunger of sailors whose ships were iced in at Point Barrow. There is the story of the monk who tossed bread over the walls of villages so that children might eat. There is the story of the Lord's Cupboard, perhaps even in your own town. In each case, the wants of the hungry were alleviated by those who lived thoughtful, sharing lives.

Questions for Discussion and Meditation

1. Where are you wasteful, and how can you correct bad habits? Have you wasted opportunities to do good?

2. In a day when certain natural resources are diminishing and when byproducts of their use are eroding life on this earth, what changes can we make in our families in our use of the earth? What changes should this congregation make?

3. In Longfellow's poem "Hiawatha," he implied that affection never was wasted. Do you think that belief is true or not? Discuss wasted opportunities or privileges. What helps you to make wise decisions? How can we help young people be useful and devoted Christians? Is there such a thing as wasted love? Explain.

WHAT'S NOT TO LIKE?
BIBLE READING: PSALM 104:5-23

The coming of summer brings forth an almost universal expression of joy. Gone are the cold winds of winter. Many decades ago on the farms of Iowa, the best part of the whole summer was when the neighborhood threshing machine began its rounds to thresh the oats. Children waited breathlessly for the sound of those huge machines coming ponderously down the road to the next farm. Women gathered in their neighbor's kitchens to put a feast on the table for the harvesters. The men, accustomed to the hard hand labor of the time, forked the bundles of oats into the thresher as they joked and told stories of other times. It was a summer festival. *What's not to like about that?*

Many of our favorite Bible stories are set in the time of harvest. We read often of the wine press and the threshing floor. Surely, the Israelites worked very hard to harvest the bounty of the earth. Wheat and barley were cut early in the summer. Other summer harvests included grapes, figs, and pomegranates. Though we usually think of harvest as a time of thankfulness with songs and shouts of joy, the summer harvest, in fact, was sometimes downright scary in early Bible times.

In spite of God's many blessings, the early Israelite people fell away from God repeatedly. During one such period, the Amalekites and the Midianites raided the fields of the Israelites during the harvest of the grain in early summer. The Israelites were finally forced to thresh their grain in the wine presses, hiding in the caves and hills to escape the raiders who came on fast-moving camels to steal the Israelite harvest. Can you imagine the labor that involved? The Israelites cut the grain by night. Instead of threshing out the kernels on the hilltops with the use of their oxen, they were forced to carry the grain to the wine presses, usually hewn from stone in a cave. Only in this way could they preserve the grain from the raids of the nomad tribes. The joyful time of summer harvest became a time of stress and apprehension.

Sound familiar? The "harvest" our children most desire after the long months of school and exacting schedules consists of sunny days of play, freedom from routine, summer ice cream cones, baseball games, and county fairs. *What's not to like about that?* Unfortunately, summer schedules might also include doctor and dental appointments, child-care arrangements, sunstroke, and the pool closing. How can we help our children go with the flow in the most positive ways? Summer can bring a harvest of new understandings, new relationships, new skills, and just plain renewal. *What's not to like about that?*

- Encourage each child to read at least one book a week. If possible, read with the child. Choose fun books, books that encourage the child's special interest, mysteries, and how-tos. Enjoy the books together, and follow through with any activities suggested by the subject matter. A book about animal life? Visit a zoo. Reading about flight? Visit an air museum, an aviary, a butterfly garden. Your child will not only polish reading skills over the summer weeks but will gain new understandings and possibly new motivation for those library visits.

- Green up your days. Summer is a wonderful time to learn more about the earth and how we as God's people bear responsibility for its care. Visit parks, forests, family farms, and corporate farms. Ask questions. How are these entities preserving God's earth? Your children have probably studied the conservation of the earth's resources in school. If possible, provide hands-on experience to reinforce that classroom learning. Encourage your family to save energy. Learn about biofuels. Visit an area where switchgrass, a possible new fuel, is grown. Think about the advantages of solar and wind power. Have your children seen a field of giant windmills? Awesome!

- Most communities from city to small town provide extra recreational opportunities in the summer. Enrolling children in swimming, golf, tennis, baseball, dance, water skiing, or other summer activities will enhance their pleasure as well as their skills. **Please do not pressure children to be experts!** It is enough to get the health benefits from physical activity as well as fun from the game and satisfaction from the new friends and coaches. **Do not overschedule children!** Be sure to allow the leisure time we all cherish.

- Summer offers special opportunities for spiritual growth. Vacation Bible school and camping programs come to mind. Sunday school is important every season of the year. (It's for Life!) Drama adds practical understanding to events and historical periods of the Bible. My grandchildren and I have practiced our sling-shooter technique on a tree, not a giant, with great satisfaction. We have survived a shipwreck in the creek and safely reached Malta by the Triple Tree. We have hiked from the Pond of Galilee to the Salt Pond. (We had to throw in the salt.) We even crossed to the other side of the creek so we would not have to walk among those dreaded Samaritans. Adding adventure, feeling the drama of the Bible story, helps us remember God's constant care of the Bible people, and of us as well.

- We love backyard treasure hunts. Children hunt for objects "that don't belong there." They may retrieve the objects only if they can name a Bible story to which it might relate. A toy stuffed lion in a tree (Daniel), small plastic animals in the sand box (Noah), a plastic fish in the birdbath (Jonah), a pipe-cleaner shepherd's staff (Moses). Twelve small stones on the deck can remind us of the twelve tribes of Israel or of the twelve disciples. A slingshot for David, a dove for the Holy Spirit, a cross for Jesus—the Bible is rich in symbols. As children collect the objects, they are reminded of treasured Bible stories and possibly hear new ones.

- One of the most important things we can do for children is to spend time with them. In some households, that time is less than ten minutes a day! With both parents working in most cases, it can be hard to find time. Doing chores together, enjoying a family hobby, sharing at least one sit-down family meal each day, attending worship and Sunday school as a family— all these cement our relationships and help our children understand and accept family values.

It does not take expensive vacations or long journeys, though these, too, can certainly make summer special. The harvest of summer joy result, first, from the loving attention of parents, grandparents, or other responsible adults. Plan for fun, plan for learning, plan for leisure, and include both guided and unguided activities. Encourage creativity, appreciate each child, and pray that God will bless each summer day. *A summer to remember—what's not to like about that?*

Questions for Discussion and Meditation

1. Read Psalm 104. What an exultant hymn of praise! Choose just three things for which you particularly praise the Lord.

2. If you and your family have taken trips in the past, spend some time remembering them together. What did we see that we especially liked? What did we learn? Did we meet some interesting people? Did we attend another church while on this trip? Did we worship at a location of magnificent natural beauty?

3. Share family goals for the summer. Is a more relaxed schedule important to you? If it is not possible for employed persons to get time off, what events will you plan that will bring a sense of relaxation and rest to all family members? Perhaps your goal is to take part in an activity you have not been able to manage as a family in the past. Can all family members enjoy this activity? Discover how other families spend summer leisure time or how they increase family time. Is there an idea you can adopt? Would it be fun to do this activity with another family from your church?

4. Many times Memorial Day is the last hectic weekend of spring. How do you celebrate, remember both our veterans and others who have died, or observe this as a "rite of passage" between spring and summer? How do you honor God on this day of national remembrance?

ARE WE THERE YET?
BIBLE READING: PROVERBS 22:6

Most parents want their children to learn values, inculcate kindness and honesty, and develop goodwill. Sometimes we ask ourselves, *Are we there yet?* Even the best of young people make mistakes. (We did, too!) *Is our job as parents ever over?* We are not to assume that parents are at fault for every mistake a child makes; we only try to do our best to guide children—and pray a lot!

There is some discussion in brain research that brains are not fully developed until people are in their early or mid-twenties. Frightening, isn't it? Suddenly, my own mother's frequent admonition to "stop and think" takes on new meaning. Most of us decide on a college, a career, perhaps marriage, certainly on patterns of behavior by the time we reach our late teens. We hope those decisions are based on solid thinking, not on impulsive behavior. As the caring adults in the lives of children and youth, we must recognize that mature decision-making may not be totally possible yet.

Helping our children control those impulsive behaviors and develop the ability to make good decisions becomes an important focus of our parenting. How does a child weigh alternatives? How much does direct experience count in learning? Does a child's faith experience have an impact on decisions and actions?

Parents are not all-wise. We must learn to balance our directives so that the child learns to choose and decide. On the other hand, the child who runs wild and receives few if any parental directives has little basis or motivation for making wise decisions. Parenting is serious business—fun and challenging—but always demanding.

Amber has little parenting. Her mother left when she was an infant. Her father works long hours, taking Amber to a babysitter at 7:00 each morning, picking her up at 7:00 in the evening. The babysitter is kind but overworked. Amber's decisions are all her own, and she is often disruptive in school and on the playground.

Theresa, on the other hand, has close supervision and few freedoms. The friends with whom she plays, the books she gets from the library, the television shows she watches, the games she is allowed to play, all are carefully screened by her parents. Every action is monitored for courtesy. Following the rules is important in this household! Theresa finds it difficult to make a decision, even taking several weeks to decide what kind of cover she wanted to make for a Sunday school booklet. Surely, there is some middle ground that would assist both Amber and Theresa to make viable decisions, even at the grammar school level.

Offering choices is probably the most effective way to start. The child, of course, must live with the choice, thereby learning that every action has consequences.

- Do you want to give your red ball or a toy car to the child who has no toys?
- Shall we have carrots or parsnips for supper?
- Would you rather go to the ball game or the park for your birthday?
- The purple socks look better, but you may wear the pink ones or the white ones, if you wish.
- If you clean your room this morning, we will have time to go to the park this afternoon.

There are dozens of such choices to make every day, and children should be a part of the decision-making when appropriate. Of course, they do not decide what kind of car will be bought or whether or not to thank Grandma for a gift.

The values we hold often reflect the community or culture in which we live. There are towns where sports are the prevailing interest, and children are urged early to excel. Other communities value the musical abilities of the children and youth; ideal is the community that nurtures its children academically and in extracurricular passions. Still, each family has its own set of values. If those are not articulated within the family, hold a family caucus to write them down.

Bible Scripture can help us. Moses, who knew more than a little about how people learn, used song and dance and word to get the message across in his last dialog with the Israelites. "Assemble the people. . . so that they may hear and learn to fear the LORD your God and to observe diligently all the words of this law, and so that their children, who have not known it, may hear and learn to fear the LORD your God" (Deuteronomy 31:12-13a). Moses wanted the Law repeated until all knew the requirements of God. Paul in the New Testament assures us that God wants God's people to possess the fruit of the Spirit, which are love, joy, peace, patience, kindness, generosity, faithfulness, gentleness, and self-control (Galatians 5:22). What a list! How can we ever teach all that?

We begin, of course, by nurturing those qualities in ourselves. Children learn much by the osmosis of a good example. Almost all of these qualities depend on the ability to listen to others, to empathize with another's problems and positions, to negotiate solutions that are fair and just. You will probably find it difficult to emphasize all of these at one time. A family, church, or community may be experiencing a situation that calls forth special qualities in its members. As you respond, share your reasoning with your children, and pray together for God's wisdom and righteousness. Openly consider possible consequences for this action. Will it help to bring justice? Will it help someone, rather than harming? Will it result in growth or in rejection? How could we do this differently to achieve better results for everyone, not just for us?

Remember that children think concretely. It is easier for them to think of direct consequences: *If I hit him on the nose, it will hurt;* rather than: *If I hit him on the nose, I am just promoting more violence.*

Growing up is not easy. Training our children in the right way is not easy either. It demands enormous effort. Maybe that is what God has in mind.

Questions for Discussion and Meditation

1. Name three family goals that you are willing to write down and post on the refrigerator.

2. What past decision do you regret? What could have been done differently?

3. What is the best decision you ever made? Was it instinctual, or did you weigh the pros and cons?

4. If your family is currently struggling with an important decision, determine whether the children will have input. How will you share the decision with all family members?

WHEN CHILDREN SPREAD THE WORD
BIBLE READING: PSALM 25:4-5

Three families busied themselves in the church kitchen, setting out plates of bread and cold cuts, bowls of leaf lettuce, mayonnaise, pickles, butter, mustard—all the fixings for a good sandwich (six hundred of them, in fact). This small church had taken on the challenge of preparing the evening sandwiches for the food pantry in the nearby city.

Soon the family members lined up before the tables in an assembly line. Dad slapped on the butter, a little girl added mayonnaise, another child chose the meat, and on they went down the line until another adult cut and neatly packaged the sandwiches. In a couple of hours, we were going out the door with baskets of sandwiches, headed for the hungry people in the city.

A great mission moment, right? Equally important is the impact of this cooperative effort on the faith formation of both children and adults as they engage in mission together. The greatest impact on the faith life of youth occurs when they are serving with other family members in acts of kindness toward others in the name of Jesus. Osmosis is important, of course: *I see adults doing good, so I will do good, too.* Children who are on the front lines, so to speak, know that they are in ministry right now; and they journey as disciples with their whole family. Christian education does not get better than this!

- A whole family in the city volunteered yard care for a single woman with physical disabilities so that she could continue to live in her condo near her work and friends. What a rich relationship has developed! The children have learned that "[Jesus] went about doing good" (Acts 10:38); and they can, too.

- Dented or slightly damaged packaged food is picked up by adults from a nearby food depot at drastically reduced cost. Back at the church, children help their families sort the food into boxes to be picked up by those who may need help. Children are not involved in the actual distribution, only in the sorting and packing.

- Parents on the Mission Committee bring their children after school to set and decorate the tables for a mission dinner, fill salt shakers and sugar bowls, and run errands.

- Two young cousins came to the Christian education office at church at least one afternoon a week. They helped in innumerable ways: setting up equipment, distributing supplies, and carrying curriculum materials to classrooms. As graduates of an after-school program, they continued to attend in order to help with recreation, music, and occasionally with learning activities. When one moved, he said, "I pray you will get along all right, but I think you will still need me." We did indeed miss both him and his mother, both members of the teaching team.

- A family with a pontoon boat hosted a Sunday school class afloat on the lake one Sunday morning. Another family provided a ski boat and instruction for afternoon fun. Doesn't sound like ministry? These were at-risk kids from a low-income area. More fortunate children learned to share and began to appreciate the circumstances of other children.

There are innumerable ways in which children can be in mission, spreading the word of Jesus through their actions as well as through their learning in Sunday school and church. Families became closer, and children developed a very distinct understanding of themselves as loving disciples of Jesus.

Questions for Discussion and Meditation

1. In what ways can your children or the children in your church family "spread the Word" about Jesus Christ in your community, church, family?

2. In what ways are you as the parent(s) or guardian(s) or church caregiver(s) providing good examples for faithful Christian living and mission?

WHAT'S THE ENVIRONMENT GOT TO DO WITH IT?
BIBLE READING: EPHESIANS 4:1-6

Looking at my brown, water-starved lawn, I breathed a prayer for rain as I turned to a detested task—cleaning closets. Just then I heard a shout of delight as my three-year-old great-grandson discovered the kittens on my deck. Legally blind, this little fellow carefully picked up a warm kitten and held it close to hear its tummy purr. Life seemed suddenly brighter as, closets forgotten, the child and I became absorbed with kitten life under the watchful eye of the mother cat.

How deeply we are affected by the environment in which we live! I watched Miles playing safely within the confines of the deck, and soon I joined him as we bumpity-bumped his toy cars across the floor. Thoughts of my brown lawn disappeared and Miles' energy zoomed as we played with kittens and cars. It was plain that this environment of fun and loving companionship was good for both of us.

How, then, does environment affect learning, faith development, creativity, acceptance, "unity of the Spirit in the bond of peace," and a host of other concerns? What can parents, grandparents, and teachers do to form environments that bring out the best in children?

I begin with two words: *Connect* and *Respect*. Children as individuals need to connect with others and with a positive environment. Each person makes a contribution to surroundings, whether realizing it or not. Life does not allow us to be a statue in a vacuum. There are ways in which we can contribute to a good environment that will nurture well-adjusted children.

In the Community

Difficult as it may seem, communities can be changed, if needed. It does not necessarily take a lot of resources, except for human resources of time and care. One community found that rowdy behavior on the town square in the evenings was keeping others from enjoying the square or even feeling safe there. A group of citizens began nightly strolls, watching and discouraging loud or unruly behavior. These citizens, under the protective eye of the police, but not employed by law enforcement, simply lent a consistent and calming presence. Things are looking up on the town square!

Another small town was suffering a minor crime wave. Break-ins were happening, tires were slashed, windows were broken, and cars were stolen for joyrides. An ex-police officer and former teacher moved to town, surveyed the situation, and decided to do something about it. He prevailed upon citizens for help and organized kids of every age into troops who picked up trash, painted curbs for the city, and engaged in useful repair work throughout town. The kids were paid for actual labor, spiffed up the town, and observed the rules of behavior set down by their leader. One person changed the environment of a whole community through gaining the trust of the children and through the help he was able to generate among other citizens.

In the Church

Children will connect with the Bible stories and respect what they teach if we teachers and parents approach the learning remembering that it applies to both us and to the students. We need to remember that we did not understand some of this in a day's time either. Children love the exciting stuff: David slaying the giant, Paul in a shipwreck, Jonah in that big fish. Why learn that stuff?

Yet even little children connect to those Bible stories. Quite often, people in the Bible were similar to most of us; God asked them to do a certain thing, and they did it the best they could. Isn't that like a child who is learning the alphabet? God means for us to be capable learners. All that a child learns in kindergarten can help the child to improve as a scholar, until someday he or she reads the Bible for himself or herself. We must keep on keeping on.

Of course, youngsters will also learn to respect and connect with others in the faith community. Every member of the congregation teaches that by the way they relate to the children and in the way the church makes and nurtures disciples. The environment of love, trust, encouragement, peace, and justice will help form faithful disciples of Jesus Christ.

In the Schools
Become personally involved with the local school system; do not leave it to someone else. Know your school board members. Vote for the ones who share your educational philosophy and recognize the importance of each child in the system. Offer your help. Make a bulletin board for a busy teacher, tutor a slow reader, help in the school library, join a parent-teacher organization to stay in touch. Sometimes, all it takes to improve the school environment for some child is a little bit of your time.

At the 110th Parent Teacher Association convention, it was pointed out that often the relationship between parent and school seems adversarial. Teachers are eager to improve any relationship that is so perceived. If you have any doubts about your child's relationship to his or her teacher, make an appointment to chat with the teacher.

Our first-grade teacher was baffled by Kenneth. She believed he had potential; but he was new in town, new in the school, and she had not been able to spark a response from Kenneth. She asked if I would help him with his reading.

Our trust grew for each other as Kenneth and I explored the school library and read many books together. It was not until we read *Annie and the Old One* by Miska Miles that Kenneth offered a bit of information. "I was born on a reservation," he said. "I lived with my grandmother until a little while ago." His grandmother, a Native American, had remained on the reservation when Kenneth came to live with his mother in our town. Kenneth was not sure he liked Iowa as well as he had liked the reservation in South Dakota.

We talked about the different cultures in which we had lived; and this led us to maps, social studies, and further sharing. Kenneth shared with his teacher and the boys and girls in his class some more information about his Native American background and his reservation life, and they were intrigued with Kenneth and his special experiences. Connecting and receiving respect from his peers made a big difference in Kenneth's life.

> *Connect and Respect.*
> *The home environment you create has a lot to do*
> *with your child's happiness, with his or her future,*
> *and with unity within the family.*

At Home

Even here we need to give attention to the school situation. If a child is having (or causing) trouble in school, that is probably happening at home as well. When you differ with the child or the child's behavior, try offering guidance rather than criticism. Super-busy families may fall into the habit of shouting or even nagging, without taking the time to help the child think through the situation and come up with a better, alternative action. Of course, there are rules to follow. A broken rule calls for disciplinary action, which must be appropriate. Children are very sensitive to what is fair; and no matter how deeply we may believe that "life isn't always fair," a child who does not experience justice will not know how to extend justice. Whatever happens to the child contributes to his understanding of the world and will influence his lifelong behavior.

In the World

Even the environment of the world can be improved a little at a time. Awareness is growing that we had better take care of this earth; it is the only one we have, and we want a green and productive earth for the generations that lie ahead. Besides, God gave this responsibility to human beings at the time of Creation, and it is time for us to take it seriously.

Children can participate in every aspect of earth-saving. They can pick up junk; walk or bike instead of asking Mom for a ride; eat leftovers in order not to waste food; limit the use of paper products, even in public restrooms; practice conservation at the park or the farm; use wind or biofuel energy when available; and make compost from grass clippings. You get the idea! Children and their parents can daily contribute toward earth preservation.

The greener, happier environment can be available for all of us. The little boy playing on my deck, and all the other children in the world, need the love, care, and justice provided by nurturing environments in home, church, and throughout the world. Equally important, children who learn to value and contribute to favorable environments will thus contribute to the elimination of violence, poverty, and injustice in the world around them. It does not get much better than that.

Questions for Discussion and Meditation

1. Reflect on the five settings in the article. What do you individually, as a family, or as a faith community do in each of these settings to improve or maintain a good environment for the children?

2. Make a tour of your home or of the church and grounds. Where are environmental improvements possible? Do you or your church use plastic water bottles? styrofoam cups? Are there danger points from unprotected outlets, discarded tools, uncut brush and brambles? Are there possible fire hazards?

3. Are Safe Sanctuaries guidelines followed in your church? Why or why not? In what ways are both children and adults protected by the guidelines?

4. Is there true "unity of the Spirit" in both your home and your congregation? What are the first steps to correcting disunity?

HOSPITALITY: WHAT'S THE FINE LINE?
BIBLE READING: 1 PETER 4:9-10

When it comes to hospitality, there was no fine line in Bible times. It was more than a custom, it was unwritten law that hospitality be offered to the stranger. In a day with few inns or other accommodations, the travelers often had to depend upon the hospitality of other desert people for their very survival. Hospitality may sometimes have been offered out of fear. (After all, who knows who these travelers my be?) Nevertheless, every traveler was offered water to drink and to bathe his feet and a bite of food.

Teaching our children to be both warm to others and safe among others is indeed a fine line in today's culture.

Hospitality today has a whole new face. We offer our welcome to our friends, our family, perhaps our work colleagues—but strangers? We warn our children against them; we are alert and often suspicious of those outside our circle of acquaintances. Teaching our children to be both warm to others and safe among others is indeed a fine line in today's culture.

A little girl escaped from the farm yard to go exploring. When her distraught Aunt Florence found her in the chicken house wearing her Uncle Ed's bedroom slippers while roosting among the hens, the child explained, "Uncle Ed says he goes to bed with the chickens. I'm going to be a chicken, too."

I think she was on to something. We do not have to be like everyone else; but if we can relate to the feelings and the habits of others, including all of God's creatures, perhaps we can begin to be hospitable and accepting. It is going to take some doing.

Sooner or later, every child will have to cope with cliques. Though schools and churches discourage them, there will always be children who form insider/outsider groups. Some of these are based on grades and activities, others simply on interests or sympathies. Often these groups hold separateness as their value, not hospitality. It seems almost impossible to break the mold, yet every Christian knows that God is impartial; God loves us all. As disciples, we seek to encourage a hospitality of heart, which requires an openness to the feelings of others.

The empathy that can lead to hospitality may develop early in children. Children who live in a hostile environment may not relate to others in a hospitable manner. Self-care is important, but not when it excludes all sympathy with the desires or needs of others. Our children may develop empathy in some of the following ways:

- Adults treat children fairly, listen to their point of view, and exhibit good manners with children. How do children feel when they are next in line at the ice cream store, but the clerk looks over their heads to take the order of the adult behind them? How does the younger child feel when a youth steals their lunch money or pushes ahead of them in line? How does the taunted child escape feelings of bitterness or inferiority? And we thought childhood was carefree! As adults, we must promptly identify and correct the injustices we observe. How else will this child experience the world as hospitable?

- Invite your child's Sunday school teacher and class to a party at your home. Urge the children to invite as guests some other child who does not go to Sunday school or have other church affiliations. These parties do not need to be either expensive or extensive. I always prepare a treasure hunt outside, a few games inside in case the weather is bad, and ask each child in the class to come prepared to suggest a game. Both the teachers and I supervise the games. I prepare simple refreshments, and we invite everyone to meet with us again at church for Sunday school. We are not only helping new children to know us and to feel comfortable with us, we are also showing the joys of hospitality to all the children.

- A distraught young woman knocked on our door in the midst of sleet and freezing rain. "I am so scared," she burst out. I urged her inside, where she told me she was on her way home from college, but the icy road had caused her car to go into a spin. Fortunately, she had skidded fully around and was able to pull into our driveway. I invited her to have a bite of supper with us and urged her to call her parents. My husband and I assured her parents that we would be glad to have her stay all night, since the roads were so hazardous. When they absolutely refused, I offered them some names to call for reference: our pastor, our physician, even our bishop! They absolutely refused and instructed our guest to get back on the road immediately. She had another 55 miles to drive on this ice. It is often difficult to receive hospitality from strangers. These concerned, conscientious parents felt that their daughter's safety was at risk, whichever way they turned. (Fortunately, when I called the parents many hours later, the young woman had arrived safely home.) When we offer hospitality to strangers, we must expect to be refused at times. This is not a rejection of hospitality itself; it is only a sign of these uncertain times and should not prevent us from doing what we can to help others be safe and welcome. I explained all of this to our young children, who included prayers for the safety of our unexpected guest at bedtime. Though we never heard from her again, we know that she was in God's care.

- A workshop was developed to help deal with difficult children in all sorts of situations. One couple introduced an intriguing and difficult problem. Their daughter was dating a boy who had become a dropout from both school and church. When the pastor attempted to call on his family, they would not discuss the situation. *Question: Should the girl be forbidden to see this teenage boy?* Weeks later, I asked whether the discussion had been helpful and what their decision had been. The girl's parents had worked out a compromise. The young man was welcome at their home anytime and often came for meals and an evening of television. However, he had to attend a youth counseling group. Gradually, he was turning his life around and planned to re-enter high school to complete his senior year. In this case, hospitality was based on a covenant.

In the post-modern world, our children are likely to meet people of all nationalities, races, and belief systems in church, school, and community. World peace, indeed survival, depends upon our children knowing and appreciating that all are created by God, all are loved by God, and all are deserving of our care. The question we ask is this: How can we show Christ-like hospitality to someone today?

Questions for Discussion and Meditation

1. Name concrete ways in which your congregation shows hospitality. In what ways could you improve your welcome? Are your ushers available for questions? Are there signs to indicate where restrooms are located? water fountains? Sunday school rooms? Is someone at the entrance to welcome Sunday school students?

2. How are your children taught to show hospitality in your home? Do you set up play dates? give informal parties occasionally? rent an appropriate movie for the neighborhood kids? Name specific ways in which your children show hospitality to others, both at home and at church.

3. When should hospitality be limited? How have you set up the guidelines? Are all family members aware of the limits? Are the limits reasonable?

PRAYING CHILDREN:

TODAY AND TOMORROW

BIBLE READING: 1 THESSALONIANS 5:16-18

Many of us remember our first prayer, lisping the familiar, "Now I lay me down to sleep." Sometimes the last two lines were changed; but even when we asked God, "If I should die before I wake, I pray the Lord my soul to take," death did not really bother us or even seem real. As a matter of fact, the thought of all those awesome and playful angels around in heaven with us seemed almost as good as a day at the park!

Prayer to a loving God, however, began to have more meaning as we spent more time in Sunday school, and especially when we began to encounter the scary realities of life as a kid. Were you frightened your first day of school? the first time you rode the ferris wheel? the day your older sibling did something really dangerous?

Or perhaps you just felt an overwhelming sense of gratefulness when you got your first bicycle, and you just had to thank God as well as Mom and Dad.

There are several kind of prayers that express our feelings to God, and children may be encouraged to be prayerful children in all kinds of circumstances. Just look to the Bible! Miriam was full of joy as she led the Israelites in prayer, song, and dance in praise of an all-powerful and all-loving God. David's heart was moved by gratefulness to our protective God when the devious King Saul was not able to put him to death. The apostle Paul sought God's direction and guidance as he tried to be faithful to his call to take word of Jesus to the Gentiles. Jesus himself went to the garden to pray when he was "greatly distressed and troubled." Each of these prayers is a response to a different reality in the life of the one who prayed. We, too, respond to the presence of God in our lives in different ways. Children in the family will not only recognize that prayer may take place at any time and for many reasons, they will be encouraged to see God in every step of daily life.

Of course, there are times when eyes-closed, hands-clasped, head-bowed prayers are appropriate. However, prayer does not always need to be formal. Spontaneous prayers may spring to our hearts in the garden, on the freeway, on the playground, before the fireplace. I have always felt that prayer time at meals ought to come after we have eaten rather than before. Who knows ahead of time how grateful we will feel to God for providing the stuff for chocolate pie, to say nothing of Mom's skill and time in making it, until we have had it?

Thankfulness, then, is one of the types of prayer that children may be encouraged to pray. It is not hard on a special occasion just to say, "Thank you, God, for the bluebirds I see by the new nest!" or "Thank God, it is spring. I did get so tired of snow last winter, God. I know that snow gives nitrogen to the soil, and I know these kids love to play in it, so thanks for winter; and thanks for spring. Your plan is good!" Just the breath of thankfulness is enough to encourage your children to gratefulness and to encourage them to express it.

Besides prayers of praise and thankfulness, there are those of petition, confession, and intercession.

It is okay to ask God for good things (Matthew 7:7-11). God is like our earthly fathers who want to give good gifts to children. Soon your children will learn that it does no good to beg for things that are not good for them! Of course, God is not going to grant harmful or even unnecessary gifts or favors. Our Heavenly Father has our best interests in mind. When we or our children ask for help to accomplish worthwhile goals, for energy to do tasks that need to be done, for guidance in making decisions, we may be sure that God responds with love and that God accepts our prayers. When in doubt, always pray! God listens to our petitions.

Prayers of confession are not easy. Forgiveness requires something more than a quick "Sorry!" Children who learn to take responsibility for their actions will realize that they must do what they can to remedy any harm they have done. My mother once sent me to school to apologize to the teacher for a misdeed, and she deputized my sisters to see that I did it! Unhappy day. It was a grudging apology at best until the teacher smiled and hugged me and said she understood. I could slay dragons for her from that day!

God, too, lovingly forgives if we express genuine remorse, accept responsibility to correct the error, and humbly confess our sin to God. Those prayers are important. Children learn that best by hearing their parents pray sincere prayers of repentance themselves.

Intercessory prayers are happy prayers. We demonstrate our confidence in God when we pray that God enter into the joys or sorrows or confusion of someone else's life and bring healing and love. Whether children pray for individuals or for nations, their caring and their prayers make an impact on the world. Just as God responded to the prayers of Moses to save the people of Israel, so God is touched by our prayers for those with cares and worries in today's world.

Often when I lead children in prayer, I ask God to grant us the courage and energy to walk as disciples of Jesus. After one "Amen," a youngster commented, "So far, so good!" We all chuckled (and I feel sure God did, too!) as we acknowledged that every day required new courage and new commitment to Jesus.

Children who pray are sure to get the help they need to deal with both the good and the unfortunate aspects of their lives. I pray that every youngster can say at the end of the day, "So far, so good, God. Please be with me."

Questions for Discussion and Meditation

1. How often do you pray with your children? your spouse? What is the role of private prayer in your life?

2. We hear often these days about "prosperity" prayers. Can we count on good fortune, wealth, or success if we pray fervently for it? Explain why God sometimes says, "No" and sometimes, "Yes," acknowledging that no one can really "explain" God. How is God's holiness evident in the answers to our prayers?

3. A group of young teenagers tipped over 164 gravestones in a town cemetery one night. For whom do we pray—the teens, their parents, the families whose tombs were desecrated, the taxpayers who pay to repair the damage, the police who failed to detect the activity? What are we praying for? Do we assess blame, ask for punishment, plead for forgiveness? Who might have been neglected? Who is the judge? Is it necessary to pray for both the victims and the perpetrators of all criminal activity, both minor and major? What would you do, how would you pray, if one of those teenagers were yours?